# The
# Weeder's
# Digest

# The
# Weeder's
# Digest

## Identifying and
## enjoying edible weeds

### GAIL HARLAND

green books

First published in 2012 by

Green Books
Dartington Space, Dartington Hall,
Totnes, Devon TQ9 6EN

Design by Jayne Jones

All photographs are by the author except the following:
page 48: *right:* Amanda Cuthbert; page 49: *bottom left:* Dave Hamilton,
*bottom right:* iStock; page 50: *left:* Gary K Smith / Alamy, *right:* Dave Hamilton;
pages 66 and 137: FloralImages / Alamy; page 142: iStock

ISBN 978 1 900322 99 7

Printed on Arctic Matt paper
by Cambrian Printers, Aberystwyth, Wales, UK

Cover image: red campion
Back cover images: *left:* oxeye daisy; *centre:* Japanese
knotweed; *right:* greater stitchwort
Page 2 image: spear thistle

Disclaimer:
Many of the foods we eat can be toxic to some degree, and particular individuals
can be allergic to almost anything. At the time of going to press, the advice and
information in this book are believed to be true and accurate. However, it is sensible
to be cautious when trying new plants to eat: make quite sure that you have identified
them correctly and try them in moderation to begin with. The author and publishers
accept no liability for actions inspired by this book.

# Contents

# Acknowledgements

I would like to thank ecologist Sue Wilson for help with identification; Chris and Jenny Seagon at Laurel Farm Herbs in Kelsale, Suffolk; Janet Bayliss and the librarians at the Ipswich Hospital medical library; and everyone at Green Books, but especially Amanda Cuthbert. Special thanks to Ashley and Jonathan for allowing occasional access to the computer, helping with computer problems, putting up with me stopping the car in random places to photograph weeds, and, of course, for tasting all the recipes.

To Ashley and Jonathan, who have come to view my trips into the garden with a colander with grave suspicion, but nevertheless stoically eat the resulting offerings.

# Introduction

"What is a weed? A plant whose virtues have not been discovered." So said Ralph Waldo Emerson in his *Fortune of the Republic* lecture of 1878 and today there are still many common plants whose virtues are not widely recognised. Wild plants are often dismissed as weeds and ruthlessly eliminated from the garden even though they may have qualities as valuable as those plants that are cultivated in their place. The large white trumpets of the familiar hedge bindweed are as beautiful as those of morning glories, and in cold northern gardens it is much easier to grow. However, while bindweed is sometimes encouraged to scramble up and cover an ugly chain-link fence, its tendency to go on the rampage means that it is understandably rarely tolerated in the well-ordered garden.

Hedge bindweed is handsome but rampant.

There is no standard botanical definition of a weed. Typing 'botanical definition of weed' into a popular internet search engine produces over a million results, but the majority of these seem to refer to the cannabis plant. The *Compact Oxford English Dictionary* definition as "a wild plant growing where it is not wanted" is probably the most widely accepted use of the word. Distinguishing between weeds and wildflowers can be particularly problematic. Some gardeners will dismiss as weeds those plants that will have others quoting from Shakespeare's *Othello*, "O thou weed, Who art so lovely fair and smell'st so sweet / That the sense aches at thee." For the purposes of this book I have included as weeds several plants which may be bought as ornamentals or grown as vegetables, but which share a tendency to spread vigorously in some situations.

Calling a person a 'weed' implies that you think he or she is puny and weak, but weeds themselves may be nothing of the sort. A mature plant of the giant hogweed will tower over most men, and Japanese knotweed quickly becomes an aggressive thug that is very difficult to control. Shakespeare did not have to worry about Japanese knotweed in the garden as it was not introduced to Britain until the 1820s. He did acknowledge the power of the weed, though, when in the play *Richard III* he had the Duke of York describe how he had heard his uncle say "Small herbs have grace; great

weeds do grow apace." Certainly the smallest root of Japanese knotweed can soon grow into a plant big enough to supply shoots for the whole family to eat.

Some weeds are avoided by people with very good reason. In North America, the very common weed poison ivy is loathed and feared by those people susceptible to its poison. The urushiol in its sap causes an allergic reaction which leads to a severe inflammation and blistering of the skin. American children soon learn the rhymes 'Leaves of three; let it be' and 'Hairy vine, no friend of mine' to remind them to avoid the plant. Children often have a greater familiarity with weeds than adults do, perhaps because they have fewer preconceptions and a greater inclination to look at the details of a plant. Generations of children have used the hairs from rose hips as an itching powder with which to play practical jokes on unsuspecting victims.

## Weeding

The majority of weed species are natives and they tend to be those which thrive in habitats disturbed by human activity – gardens, of course, being a prime example. The horsetail, whose roots go down to hell and back, and the golden sow-thistles may have been living in your garden long before anyone thought to build a house on the land. Indeed, the perennial sow-thistle is thought to be one of the first plants to recolonise the British Isles after the last ice age. The most problematic weeds in a garden, though, may well not be native, but alien species which have been introduced for their ornamental or other uses. Like the alien invaders beloved of science fiction films, these can often run rampant and prove to be very difficult to control.

Gardeners often find the problem of weed control on their patch to be overwhelming, and it can certainly be very disheartening to spend time battling with weeds only to have them reappear the moment your back is turned. However, many weeds are as nutritious to us as traditional vegetables such as spinach; indeed, the common weed fat hen and other members of the family Chenopodiaceae were valued as food, long before spinach was introduced to gardens. By viewing weeds as potential sources of food rather than of irritation, the gardener's plot becomes less of a battlefield and more a place of peace and plenty.

Not everyone hates weeding, and indeed some people find it quite therapeutic. The American President John Adams (1735-1826) once wrote that his time might have been better spent doing such things as "weeding Carrotts, picking or shelling Peas". When weeding, you are, of course, outdoors in the fresh air and if the bees are humming and the birds singing you can enjoy the natural environment while doing something active and useful. Concentrating on a relatively simple task can push any worries from your mind, if only temporarily. Weeding is a job that can be done while a large part of your mind is daydreaming about other things, although this sometimes has unfortunate results. Most gardeners will readily admit to having pulled up some prized garden plant in moments of abstraction while getting the weeding done.

Sheep's sorrel growing with black Hungarian peppers.

## Accidental and deliberate introductions

Introduced to a place where they have no natural predators, alien introductions may out-compete the native plants and become the dominant vegetation in the ecosystem. Introductions can be accidental or deliberate. Many weeds were introduced to North America by European settlers as contaminants in the grain and other crops that they took with them. Plantains are sometimes known as white-man's foot, as the seeds are easily carried on the soles of shoes, and plants have grown up wherever the settlers travelled.

Mugwort – a common wasteland plant.

Some accidental introductions have proved to be extremely invasive. Mugwort (*Artemisia vulgaris*) is thought to have been introduced to North America in ship ballast. It spread rapidly and is now considered to be one of the ten most economically harmful weeds in the eastern USA. By way of balance, there are American species that have become problematic in Europe. Canadian pondweed (*Elodea canadensis*) was first recorded in Britain in about 1836 and is now widely naturalised, often choking ponds and streams with its unrestrained growth.

Japanese knotweed is one of many plants deliberately introduced as garden ornamentals but now considered to be invasive weeds. A relative of Japanese knotweed, Russian vine is similarly robust, and is often called the mile-a-minute vine to indicate its rapid growth. Planted by those who want a quick-growing screen, Russian vine certainly achieves that aim but unfortunately does not know when to stop. Kudzu vine (*Pueraria montana* var. *lobata*), a leguminous vine from southern Japan and south-east China, was introduced for its attractive scented flowers. In parts of the USA it has gone on the rampage, twining up trees and smothering everything in its path. It is thought to cover some 2-3 million hectares (5-7.5 million acres) in the eastern USA and there are huge costs involved in its control. Unlike Russian vine, though, the nutritious young leaves and the starch in the kudzu taproot can be used. It even has potential for the production of the biofuel cellulose ethanol.

The worst deliberate introduction occurred when prickly pears (*Opuntia* spp.) were taken to Australia in 1788 by the first European settlers. Prickly pears were planted in gardens and to form hedgerows, and were used both as stock fodder and to feed the cochineal beetle, which was important for the dye industry. The suitable climate and lack of insect pests to feed on it caused an explosion of growth. By the end of the nineteenth century plants were thought to be spreading at an incredible 400,000 hectares (1 million acres) a year. When the extent of the problem was realised a massive campaign of slashing and herbicide use was started, but control was ineffective until 1926 when the cactus moth was introduced from Argentina. The caterpillar stage of the moth will feed on all *Opuntia* species and has been a very successful example of biological control.

## Living in harmony with weeds

Perhaps we should not try to eliminate edible weeds from the vegetable garden. The urge to grow plants to eat is strong and currently it is even fashionable, with many edible plants featuring in the display gardens at the top garden shows. Sales of vegetable seeds in Britain are outstripping those of ornamental plants. After all, why buy vegetables from the supermarkets and contribute towards their already healthy profits, when you can gather nutritious greens from the garden? Growing your own vegetables is usually much cheaper and you can avoid the ethical issues of using pesticides and problems with transportation.

Weeds grow where they want to be and will grow without extra inputs of water and fertilisers. Treating them as food, therefore, means that you save not only on the cost of buying seeds, but also on plant foods, and you will of

Sow-thistle growing in a herbaceous border.

course save time and effort. With increasing concern about food bills, it is certainly logical to make use of whatever edible plants are available. Using weeds as food crops does not mean that you have to sacrifice having an ornamental garden, as many have flowers and fruit that are as attractive as more conventional blooms, and they can be allowed to grow cottage-style among the borders rather than in customary rows in a vegetable patch.

## Collecting from the wild

Richard Mabey's influential book *Food for Free*, first published in 1972, did much to popularise foraging for edible plants and fungi. He encouraged people to look at the wild plants growing in their gardens and else-where as a source of food and as a way of connecting with nature, demonstrat-ing that weeds can be plants that are wanted. Roger Phillips's beautifully photographed *Wild Food* of 1983 was similarly inspiring with its intriguing recipes for ash key pickle and red clover wine. More recently Miles Irving has been doing much to bring wild plants to the attention of London's chefs with his foraging supply business and forager handbook.

To avoid any entanglements with the law, remember that in the UK it is illegal to collect plants from any Site of Special Scientific Interest or National Nature Reserve, including many protected roadside verges. It is illegal to uproot any plant, however common,

Forager Steve Brill achieved worldwide fame when he was arrested for eating a dandelion in New York's Central Park. He was handcuffed and fingerprinted and charged with removing vegetation from the park, but later released as he had eaten the evidence.

without the landowner's permission. On your own land you can harvest whatever you wish, although certain rare plants are protected under Schedule 8 of the Wildlife and Countryside Act 1981. These may not be picked, uprooted or destroyed. They include Cheddar pink (*Dianthus gratianopoli-tatttnus*) and the late spider orchid (*Ophrys fuciflora*). Orchids used to be regularly gathered for the production of salep, a flour made from the tubers, but fortunately today most people would reach for their camera on finding a rare orchid, rather than start licking their lips.

Other wild plants can indeed have you licking your lips. The intense lemony tanginess of the leaves of sheep's sorrel is literally mouth-watering. The lightly cooked flowerheads of goat's beard are delicacies to rival any culti-vated asparagus, and the first black-berry crumble of the season is always a family favourite. If the weeds in your garden seem to be getting the upper hand, try using them in the kitchen – if you can't beat them, eat them.

PART 1

# Know your weeds

# Chapter 1

# The good, the bad and the ugly

## Characteristics of weeds

A large number of plants can be classed as weeds, although, as a proportion of known plants, surprisingly few are really troublesome. Any species may be considered a weed in a garden if it grows to dominate other plants, but most weeds have a number of common features. They are usually fast-growing and able to out-compete other plants for food, light and water. They are tolerant of a variety of soils and situations. They spread readily by seed or vegetative growth. Some weeds may show resistance to herbicides and be very difficult to control.

Weeds will vary depending on the conditions in which they grow. A weed can be relatively innocuous in one garden but run rampant in another where the conditions are more to its liking. Some may be found in just a few parts of the country, whereas others, such as groundsel, may occur in virtually every garden.

Of course, as well as the weeds themselves, gardeners vary. Some people aim for a perfectly kept garden and show zero tolerance for any weeds. Other gardeners may not be so particular and can enjoy the shaggy golden flowers of dandelions without feeling the urge to leap up and grub them out. Much depends on the style of garden; weeds may be accepted in a casual orchard setting that would not be tolerated in a formal flowerbed close to the house.

Perhaps the important thing is to get to know your weeds and their characteristics and to understand which of them can be tolerated, used or even enjoyed, and which are best kept firmly under control.

Right: Hairy bittercress produces several generations a year.

## Annual weeds

Annual weeds are those such as shepherd's purse and chickweed, which complete their entire lifecycle within one year.

Some, such as hairy bittercress, are termed ephemerals, as they have a particularly short lifecycle with several generations produced in one season. Thale cress (*Arabidopsis thaliana*) has a lifespan of just four to six weeks. Its short lifecycle has proved of value in the study of molecular biology, and this species has even been grown in a shoebox-sized mini-glasshouse on the International Space Station. While its life may be short, it is certainly productive, and a single plant of thale cress can produce nearly 3,000 seeds.

The old adage 'One year's seeding means seven years' weeding' is certainly true in the case of annual weeds, and to control them it is important that they are removed before they have a chance to set seed. Many produce small light seeds that are easily distributed on the wind and are quick to germinate. The seeds can, however, lie dormant in the soil for many years until they are brought to the surface, when they will germinate and begin to grow rapidly. Annual weeds are found most often in places which are regularly cultivated or disturbed, for example arable land and in vegetable plots or on allotments. They grow rapidly and can compete with and smother slower-growing plants.

## Perennial weeds

Perennial weeds such as spear thistles are able to survive from year to year. Herbaceous perennials usually die down to ground level in the winter and survive as fleshy rootstocks or rhizomes, for example docks and stinging nettles. The roots of some species can go down to great depths in the soil, making them extremely difficult to dig out. Horsetail roots have been found at depths of 2m (6'6"). Deep-rooted perennials will usually regrow if the top is pulled up or burned off. There are also many woody-stemmed weeds, including brambles, elder and ivy. Tree seedlings such as ash and sycamore can be a particular problem in many gardens.

Perennial weeds spread by means of seed, or vegetatively, often by creeping rootstocks. Perennial weeds are often more difficult to control than annuals, as hoeing and digging may break the roots and rhizomes into pieces which are often able to regrow into individual plants. The bulbs of wild garlic may be distributed by digging or even by burrowing mammals such as rabbits. Woody weeds with thorns such as brambles and roses can be painful to deal with, as the long spiny stems need to be cut down before you can attempt to dig out the roots.

## Spreading the seed

Weeds are notorious for the prolific quantity of seeds they can produce. A single plant of shepherd's purse can produce 150,000 seeds and common purslane can produce a staggering 1,800,000 seeds per plant. The majority of these seeds lose viability quite quickly, but some can remain viable in the soil for 40 years or more, awaiting suitable conditions for germination. It is not just the quantity of seeds produced, but also the ingenious ways in which they are dispersed that enables weeds to be so successful.

## Wind

The seeds of many plants have elegant silky plumes that enable them to be carried for long distances on currents of air. The dandelion clock with its seeds surmounted by silvery hairs is the classic example of this. Other examples include thistledown, bulrushes and the fluffy seeds of the willowherbs. Tree seeds often have stiff wings enabling them to spin as they are carried along by the wind. The seeds of the ash tree, known as keys, have just one wing, whereas sycamore seeds are dispersed as two-winged pods that later split into two separate portions to release the seeds. The seeds of weeds such as poppies and corncockle develop in pods like little pepper pots and are shaken out by the wind.

## Mechanical

*Oxalis* species, hairy bittercress and many legume plants have seedpods in which great pressure builds up as the pod ripens. It then takes just the

Corncockle seed is shaken loose by the wind.

slightest touch for the pressure to release and the contents to be flung over a wide area. If you walk past heathland gorse bushes on a hot sunny day, you can often hear the explosions as the seedpods burst open. The seeds of Himalayan balsam can be dispersed 7m (23') away from the parent plant by this method.

## Water

Obviously, aquatic plants will depend on water to carry their seeds downstream to colonise new areas, but many land plants too will use water. Himalayan balsam seeds that land in water after being ejected are carried away, buoyed by the corky seed coat. The jimsonweed (*Datura stramonium*) has flat, corky seeds that float easily.

Himalayan balsam pods.

A burdock burr.

They can be carried downstream and deposited on the riverbanks, where they will germinate. The giant hogweed can also spread along riverbanks by virtue of its corky seeds.

## Birds

Many birds will cheerfully gorge themselves on the fruit of plants such as brambles and elder. They can then fly far from the parent plant and deposit the seeds complete with a neat dab of fertiliser to ensure a good start in life for the new seedling. Some birds such as jays will deliberately cache seeds, for example the nutrient-rich acorns of oak trees, for eating later. Inevitably not all these saved seeds are retrieved and many may well live to germinate in spring.

## Hitchhiking

The burrs of weeds such as burdock and goosegrass are perfectly designed to catch on the fur of passing animals, hitching a lift to pastures new. They will be spread just as efficiently by hooking themselves to the gardener's trouser legs, so it is worth paying attention if you have been working where these plants grow to ensure that you do not inadvertently spread the seeds around the garden. Seeds of plantains, flaxes (*Linum* spp.) and many mustard species become viscid when wet and will stick to the soles of shoes or the tyres of cars and so can be spread in this way. Weed seeds may be carried right across the world if they occur as contaminants in transported crop seeds, or as stowaways in trucks and ships.

## The root of the problem

Plants with a large storage root like carrots and dandelions have a taproot system consisting of one large straight root from which lateral roots may radiate. The depth of the primary root frequently exceeds the height of the plant above ground. Weeds such as grasses often build up a dense fibrous root system that consists of several branching main roots which form a mass of intermeshed lateral roots. One study[1] found that a single rye plant 50cm (1'8") tall with 80 shoot branches had a root system that equated to 210m$^2$ (2,260 sq ft) of surface area compared with just 4.5m$^2$ (48 sq ft) for the above-ground part of the plant.

Perennial weeds often have rhizomes, underground stems that usually grow through the soil close to the surface. These have buds along their length that can develop into new shoots. Weeds that spread by this method include nettles and ground elder. Plants such as silverweed spread by stolons or runners. These are a type of stem that creeps horizontally along or under the ground and forms new plants at the tip. They are similar to rhizomes, but sprout from an existing stem. Stolons typically die away once the new plant has grown, whereas rhizomes will live as long as the parent plant.

Roots that develop from organs other than the main root system are known as adventitious roots. They generally develop at the nodes of the stem. Brambles readily form roots at the tips of canes if they are in contact with moist soil. Particularly long stems that are growing along the ground may root at several places along their length, resulting in a dense thicket of plants growing around the parent plant.

Some plants, including many in the pea (legume) family such as black medick, are capable of changing

Bramble tips in contact with the soil soon produce roots.

atmospheric nitrogen gas into ammonia, a form of nitrogen that is usable by plants. This is done within the root nodules in which the bacterium *Rhizobium* lives. The bacterium actually fixes the nitrogen, in a relationship that is beneficial to the plant. When the plant dies the nitrogen is available for use by any subsequent crops grown in that soil.

## Why bother weeding?

It is not only lazy gardeners who sometimes wonder why they bother doing any weeding. Watching the bees bumbling drunkenly from one clover flower to the next, or a red admiral butterfly carefully laying its eggs on a nettle leaf, many of us may ask ourselves why we persist in struggling against weeds. Might it not be better to leave things to Mother Nature? There are, though, sound horticultural reasons why gardeners are exhorted to be vigilant about weed control.

## Competition with crops

Successful weeds are usually highly competitive, and in the race for resources our chosen garden plants or crops are often left standing. Fast-growing species such as chickweed quickly cover the soil and use up water and nutrients, while sprawling over slower-growing plants, and denying them access to light. Russian vine was introduced to many gardens as a fast-growing climbing plant, appreciated for its lacy flowers. However, it grows so quickly that it soon smothers any plant in its path. Studies looking at the effect of the weed fat hen on the growth of crops found that it was a problem in many major crops. It can grow quite tall and shade the crop plants, so even a low population can have a significant effect. When well established it could reduce yields of sugar beet by up to 48 per cent.[2]

Some weeds may show allelopathic properties. This occurs when the weed releases chemicals which can have an effect on the growth of other plants in the environment. Much of the work regarding allelopathy has been done in the laboratory rather than the field, but it certainly seems that plants such as mugwort become such successful weeds not just by out-competing other vegetation but by actually poisoning

Jack-by-the-hedge can form a dense cover.

them. Mugwort produces a mixture of terpenes, volatile chemicals which can inhibit plant growth. The roots of Japanese knotweed produce a combination of antibacterial, antifungal and phytotoxic compounds that are detrimental to the growth of other plants. Jack-by-the-hedge releases chemicals known as isothiocyanates, which inhibit seed germination and plant growth. This effect seems to have contributed to the dense stands of this weed that have developed in many parts of the USA.

The concept of allelopathy is not new. As early as 300 BC the Greek philosopher Theophrastus observed that the chickpea reduced nearby weed growth. Research is currently focused on developing crop plants that will themselves have allelopathic properties on weed growth, so that there will be less need for herbicides to control weeds in the crop.[3]

## Harbouring pests and diseases

Weeds can act as harbours for many pests and diseases. The pests can include rats and mice, who may find weed-infested areas of the garden to be ideal places to nest. Smaller pests include many insects that will feed and breed on weeds and potentially spread to ornamental or crop plants.

Weeds in the Polygonaceae family such as docks, sorrels and knotgrass (*Polygonum aviculare*) act as hosts to dock bugs. Adult bugs are seen in late spring and again from August to October. They are a brownish colour with a broad, flattened body up to 12mm (½") long and large antennae. They do not cause a problem on the dock plants, but in late summer they feed on raspberry and blackberry fruit. If disturbed they can release a pungent scent from glands on their abdomen which will taint the fruit.

Most insects are specialist feeders, with a limited range of food plants, so weeds that are closely related to crops are more likely to host the pests that attack those crops. Insects, particularly sap-sucking ones such as aphids, can also act as vectors for disease.

Dense weed growth can raise the humidity in a microclimate, increasing the incidence of many fungal diseases such as powdery mildew. Powdery mildew diseases are caused by many

Black aphids on burdock.

If you like to grow brassica vegetables – for example cabbages – it is particularly important to control weeds such as shepherd's purse, which are also members of the brassica family, as these can act as harbours for clubroot disease. This is a serious disease caused by the soil-dwelling microorganism *Plasmodiophora brassicae*. Equally, growers of sweetcorn should endeavour to control grass weeds which can act as the point of infection for fungal diseases such as rusts. Chickweed can carry the cucumber mosaic virus, which infects not just cucumbers but also lettuce, spinach and many ornamental plants. Groundsel acts as a host for several leaf rusts.

Groundsel infected with rust.

different species of fungi in the order Erysiphales. They infect a wide variety of plants including cucumbers, courgettes and many ornamentals such as phlox. Infected plants show white powdery spots on the leaves and stems, and a general weakening of growth.

## Harmful weeds

Many weeds are potentially harmful to the health of humans and to their domestic animals or pets.

**Hogweed** Hogweed (*Heracleum sphondylium*) and its big cousin giant hogweed (*H. mantegazzianum*) are both actually edible if the young spears are harvested when the flowers are forming within the leaf sheaths. Cooked as broccoli, this is a succulent vegetable with a sweet, aromatic flavour. The plants are often recommended as a suitable forager's food. However, they can also cause the unpleasant condition known as meadow dermatitis, which is characterised by reddening of the skin, swelling and the formation of large lesions and blisters. Reddening usually takes place 24 hours after contact with the plants and blistering up to 3 days later.

In 2010 a 10-year-old Irish boy had to receive a skin graft after developing severe burns from giant hogweed. The burning occurs because the sap and bristles on the stem and leaves contain furocoumarins, which make the skin hypersensitive to bright sunlight. Strong illumination and high humidity

Hogweed competing with newly planted trees.

will intensify the reaction. The fruit and roots are also phototoxic.

The dermatitis often occurs after strimming areas of rough grass in which hogweed is present, as the strimmer sprays the sap out most effectively. If you are exposed to hogweeds, you should wash and cover your skin immediately to prevent further exposure to sunlight.

Ragwort  The toxic properties of the common weed ragwort (*Senecio jacobaea*) have been widely publicised. It contains pyrrolizidine alkaloids which cause serious liver damage. Ragwort is one of the commonest causes of plant poisoning in farm animals. Cattle and horses are most frequently affected, but prolonged feeding by sheep, goats, pigs and poultry is also harmful.[4] The animals may not show symptoms until they have been eating ragwort for several weeks, but large amounts eaten at one time will cause the more rapid onset of symptoms. First signs are usually abdominal pain and diarrhoea, progressing to deterioration in general condition, photosensitisation, agitation, loss of coordination and death. There is some concern in the USA about the toxic alkaloids being found in honey in areas where ragwort is the dominant flower.

Ragwort is a member of the daisy family (Asteraceae). It has deep-green, lobed leaves and large numbers of

The daisy-like flowers of ragwort.

aconites are well-known examples. Even apparently innocuous plants such as the attractive rhododendron shrubs that have naturalised themselves in many places can produce grayanotoxins, which dramatically lower blood pressure and can even cause death. An account in Greece from the fourth century BC relates how 10,000 soldiers were poisoned by the honey of honeysuckle azalea (*Rhododendron luteum*). A more recent case occurred in Scotland when a man licked some drops of rhododendron nectar from his hand and suffered a temporary loss of coordination and inability to stand.

small daisy-like flowers of a deep-yellow colour, on plants growing 40-90cm (1'4"-3') tall. The plant has an unpleasant smell. Ragwort has a bitter taste so most horses will avoid it unless there is nothing else available to eat. However, occasionally individual animals seem to develop a taste for it and can eat it in quite large quantities. When ragwort is dried in hay the bitterness disappears but the toxic properties remain and it can then be a serious problem as the animals will eat it. Groundsel (*S. vulgaris*) contains alkaloids similar to those in ragwort but it does not usually grow in sufficient quantities to cause poisoning.

Other toxic plants Of course, many plants contain potentially deadly toxins. Foxgloves, hemlock, yew and

## Weeds and the law

In the UK, the Weeds Act 1959 classed five species as injurious weeds:
Common ragwort (*Senecio jacobaea*).
Spear thistle (*Cirsium vulgare*).
Creeping thistle (*Cirsium arvense*).
Curled dock (*Rumex crispus*).
Broad-leaved dock (*Rumex obtusifolius*).

It is not an offence to have these growing on your land but they must not be allowed to spread, particularly to agricultural land. Enforcement notices can be issued, requiring landowners to prevent the spread of these weeds. Complaints about weeds spreading to private gardens or allotments are not usually investigated by local authorities in the UK.

The 2010 Variation of Schedule 9 of the Wildlife and Countryside Act 1981 includes Himalayan balsam (*Impatiens glandulifera*), giant knotweed (*Fallopia sachalinensis*) and hybrid knotweed (*F. japonica* × *F. sachalinensis*). Again, it is not illegal to have these plants on your land, but legal action may be taken against anyone causing the spread of these species into the wild. (The inclusion of these weeds in the Act only applies in England and Wales. In Scotland, a new Code of Practice on Non-Native Species was laid before the Scottish Parliament in May 2012.)

If possible, Japanese knotweed should be burned on site; no part of the plant can be disposed of in household waste or dumped in the wild. It is classed as 'controlled waste' and as such must be disposed of safely at a licensed landfill site according to the Environmental Protection Act (Duty of Care) Regulations 1991. Soil containing knotweed roots can be regarded as contaminated and, if taken off a site, must be disposed of at a suitably licensed landfill site and buried to a depth of at least 5m (16'). It is not illegal to sell Japanese knotweed in the UK and there are several different cultivars listed in the Royal Horticultural Society's Plant Finder.

In the USA the Federal Noxious Weed Act of 1974 defines a noxious weed as "any living stage of a parasitic or other plant of a kind which is of foreign origin, is new to or not widely prevalent in the US, and can directly or indirectly injure crops, other useful plants, livestock, poultry or other interests of agriculture, including irrigation, navigation, fish and wildlife resources, or the public health" (United States Congress 1974). This legislation means that the Secretary of Agriculture can prevent species being imported, moved between states and sold if they are considered noxious; can inspect and quarantine plants; and can seize, treat, destroy and dispose of items if it is believed they have been contaminated by a noxious weed. There are more than 100 species on the Federal Noxious Weed List, including giant hogweed, rugosa rose and coltsfoot (*Tussilago farfara*).

New Zealand has strict weed legislation, including the Biosecurity Act 1993, the purpose of which is to eradicate, or effectively manage, unwanted organisms already in the country, or to prevent them from entering. Laws and regulations relating to weed control in Australia exist at the Australian state and territory government levels. The *Quarantine Act 1908* enables the Australian Quarantine and Inspection Service to physically prevent the introduction of weeds.

The presence of some invasive weeds can even have serious financial implications. In Britain many of the main banks are turning down mortgage applications for properties where Japanese knotweed is a problem. Home owners trying to sell their properties have been forced to spend significant sums of money on engaging environmental control companies to eradicate the weed, as mortgage lenders claim that it can pose a risk to the structural integrity of a building.

## Why leave them be?

Weeds in the garden are not all bad news and may actually have many beneficial effects. They are an important genetic resource for biodiversity – all our crop plants were of course originally derived from wild plants. Many weed species have important nutritional or pharmaceutical properties. Some weeds are very attractive; indeed, distinguishing a weed from an ornamental plant can be a difficult task for a gardener. The corncockle (*Agrostemma githago*), a poisonous contaminant of grain crops that generations of farmers have cursed, is much appreciated in modern gardens for its attractive flowers held on tall, willowy stems. Conversely, Japanese knotweed was introduced as an ornamental but is now feared for its ability to dominate a landscape.

### Attracting wildlife

Most wildlife sees no dilemma in the issue of weeds versus wildflowers. Native plant species may attract more wildlife, but if a plant is a good source of nectar it will soon attract insects which will feed happily without worrying about the plant's origin. Birds, too, will adapt to unusual food sources. I have watched with delight as sparrows fed on the nectar of the distinctly non-native bottlebrush shrub *Kunzea*

*baxteri* at the National Botanic Garden of Wales. Birds love the plentiful seeds provided by weed species such as grasses, fat hen, thistles, Jack-by-the-hedge and docks. Berries and hips, too – such as blackberries and rose hips – supply a rich food source for birds and many mammal species.

Butterflies find many weeds to be invaluable sources of food, in providing both nectar for the adults and leaves for the caterpillars to feed on. Larvae of white butterflies commonly feed on weeds in the brassica family, while nettles are a valuable food supply for many of the aristocrats of the butterfly world, including the red admiral, the painted lady and the peacock. Ragwort may be dangerous to livestock, but it is a vital food source for caterpillars of the day-flying cinnabar moth. The caterpillars absorb toxins from the ragwort and retain them as adult moths, making them unpalatable to predators. The common navelwort is a food plant of the rare weaver's wave moth.

Jack-by-the-hedge is a useful plant for the wildlife garden, as it is the food plant of caterpillars of the orange-tip and green-veined white butterflies. They do not compete for food as the green-veined white caterpillar feeds only on the leaves, while the orange-tip eats the flowers and developing seedpods.

The nectar-rich flowers of many other weeds attract pollinating insects to the garden. In the UK the 2007 Countryside

Survey found that changes in the way people used small areas of land are potential factors in the decline of bumblebees and other pollinating insects. Allowing white clover a place in your garden can help to encourage bumblebees and other wildlife.

Common dog violet, the most widespread of wild violets, is the primary food plant for several species of fritillary butterfly, including the high brown fritillary and the Queen of Spain fritillary.

Analysis showed that between 1990 and 2007 the number of wild plant species providing nectar for pollinators fell by up to 8 per cent. This particularly occurred in areas used for horticulture and agriculture, where on average one species of nectar-rich plant was lost in every 4m² (43 sq ft) over the 17-year period. Permitting more weeds to flower in your garden may help to reverse this trend.

Allowing a certain level of weed growth at the base of other plants, rather than insisting on bare soil, provides ground cover for predatory ground beetles and for ground-nesting bees, and birds such as the twite and skylark. Scrubby plants such as brambles and wild roses will provide safe nesting sites for many birds and

A bumblebee collecting nectar from white clover.

Dragonfly resting on a bramble stem.

perches for dragonflies, and, if dead leaves accumulate at their base, mammals such as hedgehogs may well move in.

## Protecting against pests

Allowing some weeds to remain in the garden can be beneficial if they act as sacrificial crops, attracting the attention of pests such as slugs and snails away from favoured garden plants. It may also be that a variety of plants is less appealing to the pest species than a monoculture. Beneficial weeds are generally broad-leaved plants which do not compete with crops. Studies on Brussels sprouts found that those grown among weeds had fewer aphids than those growing in bare soil.[5]

Weeds can also provide a home for insect predators, for example lacewings, whose larvae eat a variety of pests such as scale insects and aphids. There are a number of predator wasps that lay their eggs in scale insects or whitefly nymphs and moth eggs. When the eggs hatch, the larvae eat the host. Spider numbers also tend to be higher with greater weed cover, and they will help to reduce pest species.

Weeds such as crow garlic and other strongly scented plants such as French marigolds are widely recommended as useful companion plants. Their strong odour is said to mask the scent of plants such as carrots and to reduce the ability of carrot fly to find their target crop. Wild garlic is suggested as suitable ground cover under roses, and its strong aroma is thought to repel the aphids that can be such a problem when the roses put on succulent growth in spring. Extracts of the chemical allicin from garlic are currently being trialled as a cure for bleeding canker in horse chestnut trees. Allicin is known for its antibacterial properties and seems to be effective against the disease. The leaves of treated trees smell strongly of garlic, which has the side effect of repelling the leaf-mining moth  which defoliates large numbers of horse chestnuts each year.

Recent work at the former Horticultural Research International, however, suggests that scent is not necessarily important. The good effects of companion planting may simply be due to the fact that crops growing in bare, weed-free soil are more easily found by pests.

Growing crop plants with any kind of companion plants or even surrounding them with green paper makes it more difficult for the pests to find them.[6]

## Soil nutrition

Having a ground cover of weeds can help to conserve nutrients in the soil by ensuring that the ground is protected from heavy rain, which may wash away nutrients – such as nitrogen – from the soil. Weeds can also act in much the same way as mulches in reducing the water evaporation from the soil that is caused by wind. Red and white clovers are often used as a form of living mulch, and are capable of improving the humidity of the soil microclimate. The presence of weeds as ground cover in vegetable gardens, particularly during winter months, should not be considered a problem and may not adversely affect crops. In fact, weeds may help to prevent soil erosion and improve soil structure. The strong questing root systems of many weeds can penetrate hard, dense soils, improving the structure and allowing the passage of air and water.

While weeds themselves will obviously use many soil nutrients for their own benefit, deep-rooted weeds such as docks are able to accumulate nutrients from the soil that are well beyond the reach of plants with more shallow roots. When the weeds subsequently die or are removed and composted, the accumulated nutrients become available for other plants to use.

Horsetail even has the ability to accumulate gold in its tissues, as well as other minerals including cadmium, copper, lead and zinc. Some weeds which can accumulate minerals in this way, such as the alpine pennygrass (*Thlaspi caerulescens*), can be used to help remove metals such as zinc or lead from polluted soils, a process known as phytoremediation.

Weeds will also use up excess fertiliser that crop plants have not assimilated and return it in organic form; this prevents its loss from the soil and possible pollution.

Some weeds, such as ribwort plantain and wild lettuce, may act as hosts for mycorrhizal fungi. These fungi live within and around the roots and have a symbiotic relationship with the plant. The fungal mycelium will grow out of the root in search of mineral nutrients in the soil and can also colonise other susceptible roots. Both the fungi and the plants benefit from this relationship. The fungi take up nutrients from the soil, while the plant host provides the fungus with organic carbon obtained from photosynthesis. Mycorrhizae play an important role in ecosystem nutrient cycling and also protect plants against environmental stress.

In winter a covering of weeds may be useful in protecting the soil from frost, and may also allow access to parts of the garden which may otherwise become an area of mud.

# Chapter 2

# Achievable weed control

## A question of balance

A friend of mine regularly boasts that before going on holiday he ensures he has eliminated every single weed from his garden. Those of us who view weeds as a natural and not necessarily undesirable part of our gardens may never even aim to achieve this degree of control. However, if left to their own devices, some weeds will undoubtedly try to take over. It is therefore a matter of choosing what level of control you want, or can realistically achieve, in your own garden. This will, of course, depend on its size, how much time you have to spend in it, the planting style and what other plants you wish to grow. Delicate alpine plants in a rock garden will be more easily swamped by weeds than fruit trees in an orchard, for example. As with many other things in life, when it comes to considering methods of weed control, prevention is better than cure.

## Preventative methods

Many weed seeds require light in order to germinate. Trying to avoid having areas of bare soil in the garden will help to ensure that fewer weeds get a start in life. This can be done by the close planting of crop plants in the vegetable garden, or the use of ornamental ground-cover plants. Alternatively, bare soil may be mulched to deprive seeds of light.

### Crop spacing

Planting your garden plants very closely together will reduce the space and resources available for weeds. However, closely spaced crop plants will, of course, compete with each other and so it is important to allow them sufficient space for growth and for maintenance purposes.

Right: Bugle forms a dense ground cover.

Careful attention to crop spacing allows little room for weeds.

Vegetables are traditionally grown in rows, although this is not now thought to be the most efficient use of space. The plants within the rows will compete with each other for light and nutrients, and weeds will soon take advantage of the space between rows. Many studies have been done on row spacing and direction of rows in agricultural crops. The results have been variable and there are significant interactions between the different factors studied. For example, in narrow rows an east–west orientation was favourable, whereas in wide rows a north–south sowing showed better results. Narrow spacings can significantly reduce weed growth but do not always increase crop yields.

It is best to space vegetable plants so that there is the same distance between plants in the row as spacing between rows, and try to ensure they will just touch when mature. Such equidistant spacing makes optimum use of the ground. Plants that are slow to mature, such as cabbages, can be intercropped with fast-growing crops such as loose-leaf lettuces or beetroot, to ensure coverage of the soil for a greater length of time.

## Ground-cover plants

Plants that grow in thick, dense carpets are ideal for the suppression of weed germination. However, ground-cover plants should be chosen with care as some can themselves become invasive. Ivies and periwinkles, for example, will cover the ground in a dense evergreen growth but can quickly spread to other areas and may prove difficult to remove. Chinese lantern (*Physalis alkekengi* var. *franchetii*) is often planted as ground cover but can easily become a pest. Ground-cover plants are particularly useful for steep banks, as in these situations mulches would be quickly washed off in heavy rain. The dwarf juniper *Juniperus squamata* 'Blue Carpet' or cotoneasters such as *Cotoneaster dammeri* are ideal in providing erosion-resistant cover in such sites.

Ground cover can be made up of a single species, or you can create a tapestry effect by planting different cultivars of, for example, bugle or heucheras and epimediums. Sturdy spring or autumn-flowering bulbs such as narcissi or colchicums can be planted so they emerge through the ground cover to give seasonal interest. Heathers like the winter-flowering *Erica carnea* are effective in large areas. Bergenias, with glossy evergreen leaves and attractive flowers in springtime, are popular ground-cover plants, and the hardy geranium *Geranium macrorrhizum* forms a very effective cover of soft aromatic leaves with the bonus of white, pink or magenta flowers in early summer. It grows in sun or shade, and any excessive growth is easily removed and can be transplanted to another part of the garden.

Prepare the ground well before planting, and in particular endeavour to eradicate any perennial weeds first. These are difficult to remove when growing within a carpet of other plants. Newly planted ground-cover plants will require some weeding and maintenance until they start to knit together. It is a good idea to apply a loose mulch around them; this will retain soil moisture and discourage weed growth until they are well established. Established carpets of plants such as hardy geraniums can be simply mown over in late summer to keep them neat and to encourage the growth of fresh leaves for the autumn. Set your mower to its highest setting so that you do not remove the growth buds.

Of course, you may sometimes just resign yourself to the fact that a weed

Chinese lanterns can quickly fill a flower bed.

is going to be the dominant ground-cover plant in your garden. Rather than waging war with ground elder you can accept its presence, use the fresh leaves as spring greens and enjoy the lacy summer flowers. Ground elder will out-compete many border plants such as bearded irises and peonies, but there are many ornamental plants that will hold their own in its company. In my own garden the beautiful stripy rose *Rosa gallica* 'Versicolor' (commonly known as Rosa mundi) flowers profusely each year above a dense crop of ground elder. Many day lilies (*Hemerocallis*), hellebores and loosestrife will also be unfazed by the competition. *Lysimachia ephemerum* is a particular favourite as it forms dense clumps of attractive bluish-green foliage with spires of white flowers in late summer, and does not spread aggressively.

## Mulching

A mulch is any covering placed on the surface of the soil. Mulches have a number of benefits, including insulating the soil against extremes of temperature and conserving moisture by reducing water evaporation from the soil. They can stimulate beneficial soil bacteria and if incorporated into the soil they may improve the soil structure. They are also recommended as a way of smothering weeds, although garden compost and insufficiently rotted animal manures may well contain many weed seeds, which would be distinctly counterproductive.

Mulches made from bulky organic materials help to improve soil structure as they will be gradually taken into the soil by worms and are incorporated within the soil's organic matter. Suitable materials include composted bark, chopped straw, spent mushroom compost, brewery hops or coffee grounds, chopped bracken, lawn mowings or well-rotted garden compost or manures. Check with suppliers to ensure that products such as straw do not contain residual hormone weed-killer or other harmful chemicals.

To be effective, organic mulches should be kept topped up to a depth of around 10cm (4"). Established perennial weeds can grow through this, and annual weeds may seed themselves on to the surface of the mulch, but as the latter tend to root into the loose material they are usually easily removed. Do not allow mulches to build up around the stems of established plants as they can cause rotting. Organic mulches will gradually rot down and be incorporated into the soil and so will need topping up once or twice a year.

Sand, grit and gravel can also be used as mulches and are useful on heavy soil, as with time they will improve the structure. A trial at the University of Sheffield found that the number of germinating weeds was significantly reduced by a 0.5cm (less than ¼") layer of ordinary builders' sand, with a 1cm (less than ½") layer proving to be even more effective.[1] Sand and gravel

Runner beans mulched with stout polythene.

mulches are less likely to cause rotting than organic mulches and they are not thrown about by blackbirds as bark mulches are, but unfortunately cats are inclined to use them for their own purposes.

Black plastic or woven mulch materials are excellent for weed control and can also increase springtime soil temperatures by as much as 7°C (13°F), and this is useful for crops such as aubergines and peppers. In hot summers, however, they can contribute to excessive soil temperatures. While woven membranes are porous to water, in practice you usually find the water runs off rather than soaks through, so you need to check that enough water

is getting to your plants. Plants with a black plastic mulch will require especially careful watering. Pricking holes in the surface may allow water to penetrate, but can also provide an opportunity for weeds to grow through. Red plastic mulches reflect intensified red light to young plants, increasing their ability to photosynthesise, and may result in increased cropping in tomatoes and strawberries. Many plastic landscape fabrics are visually unappealing but can be covered with a thin layer of gravel or organic mulch such as chipped bark to improve their appearance. Remember that there will be an environmental impact from the production of plastic fabrics and that they must be disposed of safely when they start to degrade. It is worth considering using cardboard or thick layers of newspaper, or looking out for landscape fabrics produced from waste paper.

## Physical barriers

Invasive weeds that spread by underground rhizomes (sometimes from neighbouring properties) can sometimes be stopped in their tracks by the use of a barrier at soil level. Paving slabs or corrugated plastic or iron sheets will make straight barriers, and lengths of thick polythene can also be used sunk 50-60cm (1'8"-2') vertically into the soil. The latter will keep out weeds such as bindweed, couch grass and horsetail, but may be punctured by the sharp rhizomes of Japanese knotweed and bamboos. To control these plants industrial linoleum or specific root-control barriers are required.

Bark chips on a path in the vegetable garden.

Grass paths around beds and borders can create more work as the grasses often creep into the beds. Edging boards or a brick or paving slab around a mowing strip allows for easier maintenance. Creating raised beds for vegetables is popular and a very practical way of growing plants, making them easy to care for. Surround the beds with paths made from a woven landscape material covered with a decorative mulch of chipped bark.

## Cultivation techniques

**Thorough preparation** It is important to clear the site of all weeds before planting up a new bed or border, as perennial weeds may be impossible to eradicate from established plantings. Ground overgrown with perennial weeds can be much more work to convert into new borders than lawned areas. Set yourself a target of clearing just a small area at a time, or it is easy to become disheartened. Areas that you are unable to deal with immediately can be covered with thick black polythene or old carpets, which will kill the less persistent weeds. If you have taken on a neglected allotment it is worth arranging a work party of your friends and family to help clear the ground.

Particularly persistent perennial weeds such as horsetails may resist even repeated applications of herbicides. Laying down turf and keeping it closely mown for a few years can be the most practical method of eliminating them from the soil and a more eco-friendly option. Some vegetable crops such as potatoes have dense foliage and compete well with annual weeds, so they are often grown to help maintain clean ground for subsequent crops of onions and other less vigorous plants.

Stale seedbeds An old technique known as the stale seedbed method involves cultivating a seedbed in late winter or early spring, some weeks before you actually want to sow the seeds. Digging over and levelling the seedbed will bring many weed seeds to the surface, where they will germinate. After a couple of weeks the weed seedlings are hoed or tilled back into the soil. If time allows, the process can be repeated to allow further weeds to germinate. Timing is important to ensure that the weed seedlings are destroyed before they have chance to set seed themselves. The number of seeds present in the soil seed bank can be dramatically reduced by this method.

Careful choice of plants Choose garden plants with care, avoiding those known to be invasive; many sold as good garden plants can soon dominate if left to their own devices. Japanese anemone cultivars (*Anemone* × *hybrida*), golden rod (*Solidago canadensis*) and yellow loosestrife (*Lysimachia punctata*) are perennials which can spread rapidly from the roots once established. Red valerian (*Centranthus ruber*), bronze fennel (*Foeniculum vulgare* 'Purpureum'),

The dense foliage of potatoes suppresses weed germination.

Miss Wilmott's ghost (*Eryngium giganteum*) and euphorbias such as *Euphorbia cyparissias* are notorious for seeding themselves everywhere.

Swap plants with discretion Be careful when swapping plants with friends in case you receive something which will be too rampant in your conditions. Always check that there are no surprise extras such as *Oxalis* seedlings lurking in the pot.

Compost plants with care Some weeds that are not destined for the kitchen and have not yet set seed can go on the compost heap. Shake the soil off first to retain fertility in the bed and also to ensure the weed does not continue to grow on the compost heap. Rotary and tumbler composters are ideal for quick, hot composting; however, most domestic compost heaps do not get hot enough to kill off weed seeds. Any seeding weeds or those with perennial roots such as ground elder should not be added to the compost heap but can be sealed in damp black plastic bags for a few months to thoroughly rot down. Adding Japanese knotweed to the compost is, of course, a practice likely to end in tears.

## Manual and mechanical control

Many gardeners will find that they will need to use a range of methods to keep weeds under control, and the most usual ones are shown here.

### Hand-weeding

Many gardeners find hand-weeding to be a chore, but on a warm sunny day when the birds are singing it can actually be quite pleasurable – take a radio out with you if you are easily bored! It is better to weed for a few minutes each day than to do irregular, longer sessions. The most effective and sensitive tools to use are your fingers, but there is a large selection of other equipment available. Use a padded kneeler to protect your knees. Some gardeners like to wear gloves to protect their hands from thorns, stinging weeds and any unexpected surprises the neighbouring cats may have left in the soil.

Annual weeds are usually pulled up fairly easily by hand or with a small hand fork, as they are generally shallow-rooted. Regular weeding is necessary to ensure that they are caught before they have chance to set seed. Many ephemerals will set seed very quickly, and once they have been allowed to flower can sometimes continue to do this even if they have been uprooted and thrown on the compost heap. Weeds with weak stems such as *Oxalis* often snap, leaving the root in the ground to regrow. They are best levered up with a hand fork or trowel.

In Kipling's poem *The Glory of the Garden* he suggested that weeds can be grubbed out with broken dinner knives. They are certainly suitable and cheap, but specialist weed knives are also made; these have a hooked end and are useful for weeding along house walls or path edgings and between paving slabs. A daisy grubber is a short-handled tool with a narrow, forked blade that is designed for extracting thick-rooted weeds such as dandelions, particularly from lawns. The blade is bent into a U-shape at a point along its length which makes levering out the root easier. The Japanese soil knife or hori-hori has a wide flat blade that is useful for removing dandelions. Other spiral-type tools are available but are not necessarily any easier to use than a simple blade.

Santa's solution to the weed problem is, of course, to hoe, hoe, hoe. Several different styles of hoe are available: the Dutch hoe, also known as the push or scuffle hoe, has a metal blade set on

Annual weeds can be removed by hand.

Hoes are useful for weeding between rows.

the same plane as the handle and is used mainly for surface hoeing. The draw hoe has the blade at right angles to the handle. It is more versatile and can be used for drawing seed drills and earthing-up vegetables as well as cultivating the soil, but it requires a more stooped position so is less comfortable to use.

Diamond hoes have a diamond-shaped head on a long handle, with four sharpened edges to cut weeds on both the forward and backward strokes. The points of the blade can cut even small weeds in hard-to-reach areas.

Onion hoes are small draw-type hoes with a handle of around 30cm (1') in length, used as a hand tool for cultivating among closely spaced plants.

Hoeing is best done on sunny, windy days so that the weeds die by evaporation of moisture and will not get a

chance to root back into the soil. Run the hoe over the border or between rows of vegetables. Rosettes of annual weeds can simply be sliced from their roots or the entire plant flicked out of the soil. Hoes cannot remove deep-rooted weeds such as dandelions, but repeatedly beheading them will eventually persuade them to give up. Take care when hoeing around cultivated plants to ensure that you do not damage roots growing close to the surface.

Digging over the soil with a spade enables you to bury the weeds at depth so that they will not regrow. As they decay they will form useful humus. However, this only works satisfactorily when the soil is fairly firm, and it is hard work. Perennial rhizomatous weeds such as couch grass and ground elder will continue to grow and so ideally they should be completely removed. Of course, few of us are ideal gardeners, and in large weedy areas resorting to simply cutting all the weeds down to ground level repeatedly may weaken them sufficiently to bring them under control.

Keep hand tools sharp with a metal file and clean the blades regularly, wiping them with an oily rag to prevent them rusting. Keeping them clean prevents the spread of weed seeds and any pests and diseases that may be present. Build-up of heavy clay soil may be removed with water from a high-pressure garden hose, or by scrubbing with a firm-bristled brush. Store tools in a secure, dry shed.

## Machinery

Before using any garden machinery ensure that you have read the instructions and are wearing suitable protective clothing. Wear long trousers and stout boots, resisting any temptation to wear shorts or flip-flops.

Rotary cultivators or rotovators are powered cultivators with rotating blades. They can have special hoeing or cultivating attachments and are suitable for the mechanical removal of annual weeds in areas such as vegetable plots. However, they are not suitable for rhizomatous weeds, as they cut the rhizomes into small pieces and bury them, where they will continue to grow into new plants. Rotovators are heavy and difficult to use on clay soils, especially if the soil is moist. There are small, powered versions available for use as tillers or cultivators.

Strimmers are useful for controlling woody weeds such as brambles and young tree seedlings. There are electric and petrol models to choose from. Cutting down woody weeds will not prevent them regenerating, so for long-term control it is necessary to dig out the stumps or use herbicides on the regrowth. Applying a deep mulch may reduce the establishment of new seedlings on cleared land. Using a brushcutter makes dealing with major infestations of woody weeds easier.

Take care when strimming areas of rough ground that may contain hogweeds. The sap of all members of the Apiaceae family (also known as Umbelliferae), but especially giant hogweed, contains substances called furocoumarins. Following contact with skin, these make the skin very sensitive to light. As mentioned in Chapter 1, exposure to the sap – even for short periods – can produce reactions ranging from a mild rash to painful watery blisters which are slow to heal and may require medical treatment. The skin blistering is often referred to as 'strimmer's disease' because strimmers are notorious for spreading the sap widely. Always wear adequate protective clothing when using a strimmer, including rubber gloves and boots. A face shield is recommended.

Flame guns can be used for isolated weeds and to scorch weeds from between paving slabs and on driveways. They will also kill any weed seeds on the surface. Use them when the foliage is dry and be sure to allow sufficient burn-time to kill deeper-rooted weeds. There are various types; some use paraffin and others have a butane gas cylinder. Check on an out-of-the-way corner to make sure that the flame will not scorch the paving slabs. Do not use on windy days in case you inadvertently burn cultivated plants.

## Biological weed control

Biological weed control involves the use of any biological organism to attack weeds. At its simplest it could consist of using a few chickens to clear the weeds in an area of garden. Chickens are very effective weeders and will eat not just the green, living weeds, but also any seeds and insects they find while scratching in the ground. However, they are not neces-sarily selective, and may well decide that they want to try some of your favourite plants, or may scratch around and dustbathe in new seedbeds. If you have free-range chickens you may have to protect newly planted seedlings with bamboo cloches or circles of chicken wire. Alternatively, you can keep the chickens in an ark with a moveable run, and just move the run to wherever you require some weeding to be done.

Geese will eat weed grasses and have been used to weed in between rows of established crops. They double up as very effective guards and are great personalities. A team of KellyBronze

Chickens will eat many different weeds.

turkeys has been used as organic strimmers in grassland areas of the Hyde Hall estate in Essex. They spend the day foraging among the weeds and grasses and roost in trees at night.

Sheep are useful for weed control as they graze close to the ground and will eat a wide range of plants. Goats are browsers and will help to control woody weeds. If you have a large area of land to clear, though, then the pig is really the best ally you can find. Pigs, particularly traditional breeds such as the Tamworth, are excellent at rooting out the succulent underground portions of weeds and will eat virtually anything. They have even been used to clear poison ivy. However, some plants such as hemlock, horseradish and white bryony will cause poisoning, so land must be checked before allowing the animals on it. Pig-keeping must not be undertaken lightly, and the pigs must be securely fenced. Many countries have strict rules on the keeping and moving of pigs and other livestock, so check with your local Department of Agriculture if you are considering keeping them.

The term 'biological weed control' usually refers to the release of an organism, normally a fungus or an insect, that attacks weeds. The biological agent may not necessarily kill the target weed, but should at least reduce its ability to compete with crops and prevent it setting seed. Extensive research is now required before any bio-control agents are introduced, to ensure that the introduced organisms only affect the target pest. The introduction of a biological control agent may not actually be deliberate. A fungal rust, *Puccinia lagenophorae*, which is of Australian origin, has become established on groundsel plants in France and the UK since the 1960s. It reduces the viability of groundsel plants on which it is found.

As mentioned in the Introduction, the caterpillars of the cactus moth rapidly devour prickly pear, and so successfully that in Dalby, Queensland, a monument was dedicated to the moth. A sap-sucking plant louse found in Japan is currently under assessment as a bio-control agent for Japanese knotweed.

## Herbicides

Herbicides are chemicals that kill plants and they are regularly used for weed control. They are generally indiscriminate in their actions, though, and many will leave residues in the soil so they should be used with care. Long-term use of herbicides can result in weeds developing resistance to them.

Very few herbicides are suitable for organic growers. There are various products based on concentrated food-grade acids, for example 20 per cent acetic acid or citric acid (as opposed to the 5 per cent acetic acid in household vinegar). They work by burning the waxy cuticle off the foliage of the plant. Like products based on pelargonic acid they cause rapid dehydration of the weeds and leave no harmful residues, but are non-selective.

Contact herbicides are non-selective chemicals and work simply by scorching off weed foliage. They are useful for controlling annual weeds and will kill perennial weed seedlings, so can be used to clear ground prior to sowing or planting. Contact herbicides will only kill when in contact with the foliage, so bulbs underground or tree roots nearby will be unharmed.

Systemic herbicides such as glyphosate are also non-selective. They differ from contact herbicides in that when applied to the leaves, the chemical is carried down into the root system of the weed, making it effective in

Creeping thistle after being sprayed with a hormone weedkiller.

controlling deep-rooted perennial weeds.

Residual herbicides are long-lasting chemicals that can remain in the soil for several months. They can also be referred to as pre-emergence herbicides, because they will kill germinating seedlings as they emerge. They are sometimes used to maintain weed-free strips at the edges of gardens, as they are able to keep creeping weeds at bay.

When using herbicides it is important to follow all the instructions on the manufacturer's label and to apply the chemical at the stated rate and in the manner described. It is a legal requirement to comply with the statutory conditions indicated.

For thorough weed control make sure you are spraying at the correct times and intervals. If using a dilutable product rather than a ready-to-use formulation, try to make up only sufficient solution for the job required. Left-over spray must not be poured down the drain nor left where children can reach it; check with your local council for advice on disposal of hazardous waste.

**CAUTION: APPLYING HERBICIDES SAFELY.** When applying chemicals, avoid contact with exposed parts of the body, particularly the eyes. Avoid breathing in sprays and wash any splashes off the skin immediately with clean water. Make sure no children or animals are in the vicinity when spraying. Do not spray in windy or very sunny weather. Spray to thoroughly wet the plants but without excessive run-off or drift, clean all equipment well after spraying and wash any exposed skin. Once you have used a watering can or sprayer for weedkiller, keep it just for that use in case residues of the chemical cling to the container. Store all chemicals in a safe place, away from children and animals, keeping them in their original containers and tightly sealed. If you possess any out-of-date chemicals, contact your local authority's waste disposal section for advice on suitable disposal sites.

# Chapter 3

# A case of mistaken identity

## Poisonous plants

Poison control centres in many countries receive large numbers of telephone calls asking for information about plants. The actual number of cases of confirmed plant poisonings, though, is very small. The few deadly poisonous plants that exist are generally well known in the areas in which they grow, and are avoided. As with cases of fungi poisonings, plant poisonings are most likely to occur when a person has mistaken a poisonous species for an edible one.

### Dog's mercury (*Mercurialis perennis*)

One plant which seems to cause confusion is dog's mercury. A member of the spurge family (Euphorbiaceae), it is a very common woodland plant, often forming the dominant ground vegetation in the shade of trees. A case was reported in the *British Medical Journal* in 1983 in which a 40-year-old schoolmaster and his wife ate a large quantity of dog's mercury, which they had mistakenly identified as the edible plant brooklime. They both presented

Dog's mercury is common in woodlands.

Brooklime, with its attractive blue flowers, is fairly easy to identify.

to hospital seriously ill with nausea, vomiting and severe colicky pains.[1] The vegetable writer Joy Larkcom has also described how acquaintances had mistaken dog's mercury for ground elder and were hospitalised as a result.

Dog's mercury has been known to be very poisonous since at least the seventeenth century, when the herbalist Nicholas Culpeper wrote "There is not a more fatal plant, native of our country than this species of mercury." To those who know the plant, mistaking it for brooklime or ground elder seems unlikely, but if the plants are not

**❶ CAUTION:** It is absolutely essential that you identify any plant accurately before eating it, as there are a few edible species that may be confused with poisonous plants. Plants often vary in appearance depending on the season and growing conditions, so it is important that you do not rely on a single picture from a book. Use a good botanical text or, better still, attend a course and be guided by an expert.

Ground elder has divided leaves.

Deadly nightshade is appropriately named.

in flower there are certain similarities. Dog's mercury has dark green leaves in opposite pairs.; they are simple ovals and slightly pointed. The green flowers are tiny and grow on erect spikes. Brooklime also has opposite pairs of leaves, but is an altogether fleshier plant with startling blue flowers. Ground elder has leaves that are divided into several leaflets and it has umbels of white flowers.

## Deadly nightshade (*Atropa belladonna*)

The deadly nightshade is another plant that has been mistaken for edible species. It is a member of the Solanaceae family, which includes potatoes and tomatoes. The generic name *Atropa* comes from Atropos, the name of the Greek goddess of the underworld who cut the thread of life. The specific name *belladonna* is from the Italian for 'beautiful woman' and is thought to refer to the pupil-dilating effect of the atropine toxin. Most cases of poisoning from deadly nightshade occur when children eat the glossy black berries, but they have also been eaten stewed by a family who mistook them for bilberries. In Germany there have been two cases of adults who had gathered the green leaves and boiled them as a vegetable.

Edible plants can of course have non-edible parts. Potatoes contain solanine, which is also present in their relative, the deadly nightshade. The toxin affects the nervous system causing headaches, digestive disturbances, confusion, coma and death. Fortunately, levels in cultivated potatoes are very low, although they increase as the tubers age or if they are damaged or exposed to light. For this reason green potatoes should not be eaten.

Like the Solanaceae, the carrot family (Apiaceae) contains edible members such as the wild carrot (*Daucus carota*) as well as some that are toxic. Members of the family are commonly called umbellifers, as the flowers are in the form of an umbel, a word that has the same root as that of 'umbrella'. They include many common vegetable and herb plants such as carrot, parsnip, celery, parsley and caraway. Unfortunately, the group also includes some of the most poisonous of all plants and you must take great care with identifying all umbellifers, especially those growing near water.

Hemlock stems are marked with purple.

## Hemlock (*Conium maculatum*)

Hemlock is well known as the source of the poison used by the Greeks for the execution of Socrates in 399 BC. It can be found on roadsides, the edges of fields and in damp woodland. It is usually a biennial plant, growing up to 2.5m (8') tall, with delicate ferny leaves and umbels of white flowers. It can be distinguished by irregular purple blotches on the stem and the unpleasant mousy smell of the crushed leaves. However, people have died when they have mistaken it for similar plants such as wild carrot or parsley, as even small quantities are poisonous.

Wild carrot (left) and parsley (right) in flower. Both bear a resemblance to hemlock.

## Cowbane (*Cicuta virosa*)

Cowbane is not as widespread as hemlock, but plants can be numerous where conditions are to its liking. It is found in wet conditions such as ditches or riverbanks, or at the edges of ponds. Cowbane has elongated leaflets and typical white umbels of flowers, and a smell reminiscent of celery. The thick, fleshy white tubers contain a series of hollow chambers. Cowbane is extremely poisonous and even a few mouthfuls can result in death.

## Hemlock water dropwort (*Oenanthe crocata*)

Also growing in wet areas is hemlock water dropwort, sometimes called dead men's fingers on account of the clusters of white or yellowish tubers found at the base of the stems. Hemlock water dropwort is thought to be the herb used by Phoenician colonists on Sardinia to intoxicate criminals and elderly people who could no longer look after themselves, before they were ritually killed by being dropped from a high rock or beaten to death. The toxins in hemlock water dropwort cause symptoms including facial paralysis and the so-called sardonic grin described by Homer in the eighth century BC.[2]

Unlike many other poisonous plants, which can have a bitter taste, the tubers of hemlock water dropwort are said to taste quite pleasant. Oenanthe-toxin is found in all parts of the plant and especially in the roots, and causes death in more than half of the cases of poisoning by this species. Most cases arise from people confusing the plant with other umbellifers, and this emphasises the importance of identifying this group of plants correctly. If in any doubt, do not eat them.

Cowbane growing on a riverbank.

Hemlock water dropwort.

**❶ CAUTION: WHAT TO DO IF SOMEONE HAS CONSUMED A POISONOUS PLANT. If you are concerned that someone may have eaten a poisonous plant, consult a doctor or your nearest hospital as soon as possible. Most major hospitals will have a poison control centre and in the UK all hospitals, general practitioners and other health care workers have direct access to the clinical toxicology database TOXBASE. If attending hospital try to take along a sample of any suspect plants. When submitting plants for identification it is important to collect specimens of the entire plant, including the roots. Wet newspaper should be wrapped around the roots of the specimen, which should be placed in a plastic bag to keep it from drying out.**

## Toxins in everyday food plants

Many everyday food plants contain toxins which are not a problem as they are only consumed in small amounts. The pips of apples, for example, contain low doses of amygdalin. Eating a couple of apples with their pips is not harmful, but consuming a teacupful of apple pips could cause cyanide poisoning. Individual sensitivities to toxins will vary and some people can be quite unaffected by doses that can make others seriously ill. There are still isolated cases of poisoning by plants that were previously unsuspected of being toxic, so just because a plant is listed as edible does not mean that it will never cause problems with any individual. When trying something new it is always wise to have a very small portion initially and see if that has any detrimental effects.

Oxalic acid and its salts, known as oxalates, are naturally occurring chemicals present in most commonly eaten plants, including cereal grains, spinach and beets. Some plants, however, can contain potentially toxic quantities of oxalates. The rhubarb plant is a well-known example of this. Rhubarb is a popular ingredient in many spring desserts such as crumbles and fools, and can also be eaten in savoury dishes, working well with rich, fatty foods such as duck or mackerel. The edible stems can usually be eaten regularly without causing problems. For example, Alan Bloom – the famous horticulturalist who started Bressingham Gardens in Norfolk – ascribed his advanced age to eating rhubarb for breakfast regularly. He lived to be 98, so certainly seemed to do well on it.

However, eating excessive quantities of rhubarb stems can lead to calcium oxalate crystals being deposited in various tissues, especially the kidneys, causing kidney stones, which are excruciatingly painful. The leaves of rhubarb contain much higher quantities of oxalates than the stems, and so eating even small amounts may cause problems. Animals grazing on large quantities of plants rich in oxalates can develop the condition known as milk fever. The oxalates lock up vital soluble calcium as the non-soluble calcium oxalate, leading to hypocalcaemia, symptoms of which include staggering and convulsions. Some plants, such as the alpine willowherb *Epilobium glabellum*, found in New Zealand, have leaves filled with sharp needle-shaped crystals of calcium oxalate that deter grazing animals from eating them.

The formation of calcium oxalate stones is not wholly understood and depends not just on the dietary oxalates consumed, but also on levels of ascorbic acid (vitamin C) and calcium in the diet; low calcium intakes increase the risk of stone formation.[3] Many lists of oxalate levels in foods are not reliable.[4] Individual responses will also vary, making it difficult to make specific recommendations.

**CAUTION:** It is probably wise to restrict portion sizes of high-oxalate plants such as sorrel, fat hen, orache and other members of the Chenopodiaceae to around 100g (3½oz) per person and to serve them no more than 2-3 times a week.

Saponins are widely distributed in plants including many that we eat every day, such as legumes, spinach and other foods such as oats and red wine, as well as in plants including horse chestnuts and cyclamen, and weeds such as campions. They derive their name from the Latin *sapo* (meaning soap), a word also reflected in the Latin name for soapwort, *Saponaria officinalis*. Saponins have a bitter taste and produce a soap-like foam when shaken with water. They are poorly absorbed by the body and are generally harmless to mammals, but can be toxic if eaten in large quantities, causing digestive disorders. They also have the ability to haemolyse red blood cells, although are broken down by cooking.

All plants will absorb nitrates from the soil and can sometimes accumulate quite high concentrations of them, particularly where there have been high levels of nitrate fertilisation. Wild lettuce (*Lactuca virosa*) may contain elevated nitrate levels under certain conditions such as lack of light or a deficiency of the essential micronutrients molybdenum and iron. Nitrates in themselves are not usually a cause for worry, but they can be converted by gut bacteria into nitrites, which are more toxic. These combine with haemoglobin in the red blood cells and can prevent the uptake of oxygen. Nitrate levels have been considered an area of concern for some years, but recent studies seem to be suggesting that the nitrates in vegetables such as beetroot may actually be beneficial in lowering blood pressure.

It is important to consider where you gather the weeds that you eat. In your own garden you will be aware if any chemicals have been used that could contaminate plants, but you should be particularly careful of gathering weeds from roadsides, where they may have become contaminated with heavy metals or other pollutants. Research on soil from 35 sites in the north of England found that levels of heavy metals in roadside soils were higher as compared to their natural background levels in British soils, with lead concentration being the highest, ranging from 25μg/g to 1198μg/g. However, levels were below what are known as the 'critical trigger concentrations' for the contaminated soils.[5] Former industrial and other brownfield sites may have contaminated soil, and plants growing there should be treated with caution. Many councils regularly spray verges with herbicide, and depending on the product used the effects may not be instantly noticeable.

As with other food items, edible weeds can sometimes prove to be harmful to a few individuals. This does not mean that everyone should stop eating them. After all, some people are strongly allergic to strawberries, but it is not necessary that everyone avoids the fruit, as the vast majority of the population can eat them safely. There have been isolated cases of allergies to some common weeds. Dandelions, for example, have a milky sap which contains latex, which can cause a contact dermatitis in people who are allergic to latex.

Spending time getting to know the wild plants that grow around you is the best way to learn which ones you can safely use. Observe the leaves and how they connect to the stem. Pick a handful of leaves, crush them and smell them. Visit them regularly to watch a flower unfold and return to see the fruit develop – take some indoors and compare them with pictures in books or on the internet. Gradually you will develop a familiarity with them. We all have busy lives today and it may be difficult to spend time making friends with plants, but, as with human friendships, doing so can enrich our lives.

There are some plants that are still traditionally eaten in some parts of the world but are now known to be harmful. I have included these borderline-poisonous plants – for example, bracken – in Part 2 of this book, since, as they are sometimes eaten, it is important that people are aware of the facts about their consumption. However, it is essential that you understand the potential dangers of trying them yourself.

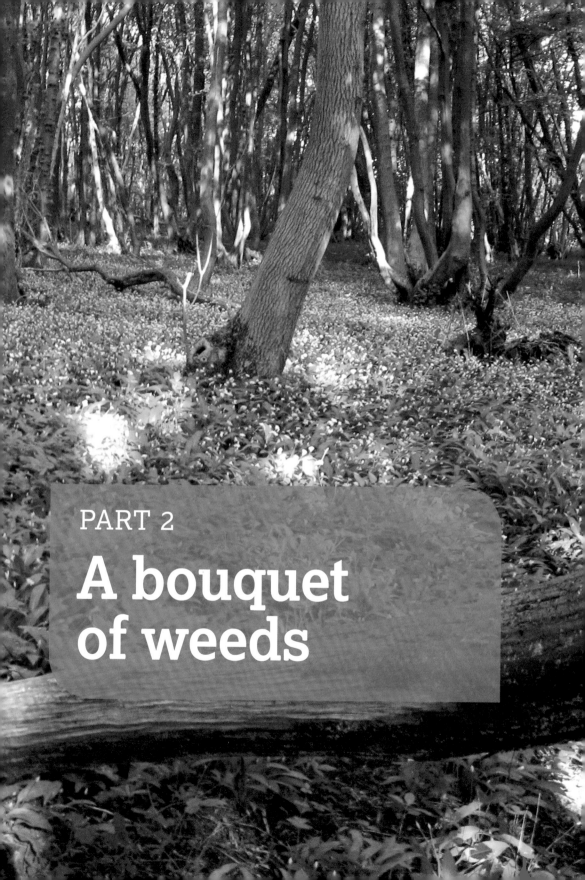

PART 2

# A bouquet of weeds

# Alexanders
## (*Smyrnium olusatrum*)

Native to the Mediterranean region, the parsley of Alexandria was a popular spring vegetable and is thought to have been introduced to Britain by the Romans. It was frequently grown in monastic herb gardens as a pot-herb and sometimes remains on such sites long after the monks have gone. It survives on the island of Steep Holm in the Bristol Channel, along with a few plants of the beautiful peony *Paeonia mascula*, which was cultivated for its supposed medicinal properties. In her *Book of Household Management* (1859-61), Mrs Beeton suggested that Alexanders be used in the same way as celery but said that "its cultivation is now almost entirely abandoned". The leaves and stems of Alexanders contain more vitamin B1 (thiamine) weight-for-weight than do potatoes. They are also a useful source of vitamin C.

## Appearance and habitat

Alexanders generally grows near the coast and is naturalised on cliffs, roadsides and hedgerows. Once you recognise the plant, you will find it easy to spot with its handsome, very shiny dark green leaves and tall robust stems to 1.5m (5'), bearing umbels of yellowish-green flowers. It is a biennial plant, growing one year and flowering from April to June the next. It emerges very early in the year. The glossy leaves, held in groups of three, are resistant to frost.

## Uses

The leaves of Alexanders have a somewhat pungent taste, similar to the herb angelica, although the Latin name *Smyrnium* implies that they have a myrrh-like smell. Use a few young leaves raw to add interest to a mixed salad. The taste becomes milder on boiling leaves in water, and they are useful for early spring or Lenten greens, to make a green sauce for fish (in the same way as Jack-by-the-hedge is used, see page 121) and for adding to soups and stews. In Versailles in the eighteenth century they were blanched to use in winter salads.

The young stem bases are quite succulent, and when cooked and served with melted butter as you would asparagus, they can be a delicacy. Cut the stems low to the ground, using the bottom 15cm (6") or so, where they have usually been blanched by the surrounding vegetation and their own leaf bases. Stems become hollow with age. Boil them for just 5 minutes and serve immediately.

The flowerheads, which open like miniature cauliflowers, can be dipped into tempura batter to make savoury fritters, or pickled while in bud. The carrot-like roots can be dug up for winter soups and the large black seeds add an interesting flavour to risottos, or ground to make a pepper substitute.

## Related plants

Alexanders is a member of the Apiaceae (Umbelliferae) family, which includes many edible plants including carrots, celery and parsnips, and herbs such as dill, fennel and angelica.

> **CAUTION: There are some very poisonous family members such as cowbane and hemlock (see pages 49 and 50), so do be careful to ensure that you can identify the plants correctly.**

## Pickled Alexanders

Approximate preparation time: 1 hour

1 jugful Alexanders flower buds
1 tbsp peppercorns
30g (1oz) ginger root, peeled and grated
30g (1oz) salt
285ml (10fl oz / ½ pint) white wine vinegar

1  Blanch the flower buds in boiling water for a few seconds. Drain and allow to cool.

2  Fill a sterilised Kilner jar with the buds, peppercorns and ginger.

3  Stir the salt into the vinegar, pour into the jar and seal. Let the flavours develop for a few days before using. The alexanders should keep in a refrigerator for several months, so long as they are fully immersed in the vinegar.

# Black mustard
## (*Brassica nigra*)

An annual member of the brassica family, black mustard has been cultivated for its seeds for thousands of years. The ancient Egyptians were said to have crunched the seeds during meals to aid digestion. In Victorian times mustard was widely used, not just as a condiment but also medicinally in poultices and, in mustard baths, used to soak the feet as a way of warding off colds. Mustard seed has a high oil and protein content. The oil is mostly in the form of monounsaturated fatty acids, which are thought to have a protective effect against coronary heart disease.

## Appearance and habitat

Black mustard occurs chiefly as a weed on roadsides, riverbanks and waste ground. It is a tall plant growing to 1m (3') or more. The leaves are held on stalks and the bristly bases of the leaves are divided into leaflets. As with many members of the brassica family, the four-petalled flowers are a rich yellow.

## Uses

The seeds usually ripen in August and September. Collecting enough to be useful is a fairly laborious process, but it is the sort of task that can be given to bored schoolchildren in the long summer holidays. They are probably more likely to be motivated to do the job if you can provide a cannonball with which to crush the seeds afterwards, as suggested by one eighteenth-century cookbook author. For those not suitably equipped, the seeds can be ground with a pestle and mortar, or even a coffee grinder if you do not mind cleaning it thoroughly afterwards.

To make mustard, moisten the ground mustard with water then add a pinch of salt and sufficient white wine vinegar to give the required consistency. It can be flavoured with tarragon or horseradish for extra punch. Store in the refrigerator, but use as soon as possible as it loses potency with age.

The seeds can be used whole in pickles, relishes and chutneys such as piccalilli or added to egg or cheese dishes. The Italian *mostarda di frutta* is a confection of candied fruit in a mustard syrup, served with boiled meats or cheeses in northern Italy.

Charlock, an edible relative of mustard.

include charlock (*S. arvensis*), whose bitter leaves are sometimes eaten as spring greens, and oil-seed rape, which often self-seeds on road verges.

## Related plants

White mustard, *Sinapis alba*, is milder in taste than black mustard. Most commercial mustards use a blend of the two types of seeds; it is the white mustard seed that is sprouted for mustard and cress. Other wild yellow-flowered brassicas which may be found

**CAUTION: Mustard oil can be a skin irritant and, if taken to excess, can cause enlargement of the thyroid gland (a condition known as goitre).**

## Tomato and mustard-seed chutney

Makes about 6 jars
Approximate preparation time: 1 hour, plus storage time

900g (2lb) green or red tomatoes, chopped
900g (2lb) cooking apples, peeled and chopped
400g (14oz) onions, chopped
200g (7oz) sultanas
400g (14oz) brown sugar
30g (1oz) mustard seeds
900ml (30fl oz / 1½ pints) malt vinegar
1 tsp paprika

1 tsp ginger
1 tsp turmeric
2 tsp salt

1  Put all the ingredients into a heavy-based saucepan and simmer gently until thick and soft (around 30-40 minutes).

2  Spoon into sterile glass jars, seal, and leave to mature for a couple of weeks before using.

# Blackberry
## (*Rubus fruticosus* agg.)

*Rubus fruticosus* is an aggregate name for a number of different but similar species. Botanists think that there may be as many as 2,000 different species of bramble in Europe. However, from the point of view of the gardener struggling with the thorny stems that have infiltrated his or her flower beds, or the child eating fruit from the hedgerow, they are all blackberries or brambles. The blackberry is probably the most widely known of wild foods, and family trips to the countryside in early autumn to gather the fruit are still enjoyed by many.

In his book *Flora Britannica*, Richard Mabey reports that the stems were once called lawyers "because of the trouble you have escaping if you happen to fall into their clutches". Folklore decrees that blackberries should not be picked after 'Devil's blackberry day', which is variously said to be on or around 13th October. This is meant to be the day on which the Devil was thrown out of heaven and landed in a prickly blackberry bush. He spat on the bush and so any fruit eaten after this day tastes bitter. It is certainly true that fruit gathered late in the season can taste unpleasant but this is more likely to be due to the growth of mildew on the berries and the presence of maggots.

The aromatic berries have been eaten by humans for thousands of years. They are a good source of many vitamins, including vitamin C, and are rich in antioxidants. Wild berries have a higher antioxidant content than cultivated ones.[1] The seeds are rich in omega-3 fatty acids, which may help to prevent heart disease.

## Appearance and habitat

Blackberries are shrubby plants which can be evergreen or deciduous. They have long, upright or trailing stems known as canes, which can reach as much as 9m (30') in length, and roots can form wherever the stem touches the soil. The stems are armed with sharp thorns which deter grazing animals and help the stems cling on to other vegetation.

Cut unwanted blackberry canes back to prevent them forming roots where they touch the soil, and dig out the roots as soon as you see them. Otherwise, you can have a bramble thicket establishing itself before you know it.

## Uses

Blackberries are often eaten straight off the bush or taken home to be eaten raw with cream, and are best consumed on the day they are picked or some of the flavour is lost. They are used in many different cake and dessert recipes and are particularly good when partnered with apple. Invaluable for classic autumn puddings such as crumbles, the rich aromatic taste is excellent in preserves and cordials and makes a wonderful liqueur.

Blackberry leaves are also said to be edible, but even when very young are quite high in tannins, so taste astringent and are difficult to digest. However, a tea made by infusing fresh or dried leaves in just-boiled water for 5 minutes is soothing and has been used in the past as a remedy for upset stomachs.

Young shoots, harvested just as they are emerging from the ground in spring, are said to have been used as a substitute for asparagus (although in truth they do not taste anything like it!).

### Blackberry crowdie

Serves about 2
Approximate preparation time: 30 minutes

4 tbsp rolled oats
Knob of butter
170ml (6fl oz) double cream
2 tbsp honey
1 tbsp whisky
1 cup blackberries

1  In a saucepan, lightly brown the oats in the butter. Remove from heat and allow to cool.

2  Beat the cream until soft peaks form. Stir in honey and the whisky.

3  Fold in the browned oats. Layer the berries and cream mixture in tall glasses, finishing with a few berries.

# Blackberry jelly

Approximate preparation time: 1 hour, plus straining overnight

1kg (2lb 3oz) blackberries
1 large cooking apple, roughly chopped
140ml (5fl oz / ¼ pint) water
Sugar

1  Put the blackberries and apple into a pan with the water. Simmer gently for around 20 minutes until the fruit is very soft.

2  Strain though a jelly bag overnight.

3  Measure the juice into a clean pan. For every 570ml (20fl oz / 1 pint) juice add 400g (14oz) sugar.

4  Stir over a gentle heat until the sugar has dissolved. Bring to the boil and boil rapidly for about 10 minutes until setting point is reached. To test for setting, drop some jam on to a cold saucer. Let it cool slightly then gently push the surface; if it wrinkles it is ready. Pour into sterile jars and seal.

# Blackberry brownies

Approximate preparation time: 45 minutes

200g (7oz) dark chocolate
100g (3½oz) butter
200g (7oz) sugar
200g (7oz) self-raising flour
2 eggs
100g (3½oz) blackberries
100g (3½oz) chocolate chips

1  Melt chocolate, butter and sugar together in a saucepan over a very gentle heat.

2  With a wooden spoon mix in the flour and eggs and then the blackberries and chocolate chips.

3  Pour into a baking tray approximately 20×25cm (8"×10") and bake in a

medium oven (180°C / 350°F / Gas Mark 4) for around 30 minutes until set. Cut into 20 squares or 12 piggy portions.

# Blackberry and apple crumble

Serves 6
Approximate preparation time: 1 hour

680g (1lb 8oz) blackberries, rinsed
and drained

680g (1lb 8oz) apples, peeled, cored
and sliced

2 tbsp demerara sugar

Knob of butter

*For the crumble topping:*

100g (3½oz) butter

200g (7oz) plain flour

50g (1¾oz) rolled oats

50g (1¾oz) sugar

1 tsp cinnamon

**1**  Put fruit, sugar and knob of butter in
a pan and cook gently until the apples
start to soften.

**2**  Transfer the fruit and a few tablespoons of the resulting juice to an
ovenproof dish around 20×25cm
(8"×10").

**3**  To make the crumble, rub the butter
into the flour until it is the consistency
of breadcrumbs. Stir in the oats, sugar
and spice, and sprinkle topping over
the fruit.

**4**  Bake in a hot oven (220°C / 425°F /
Gas Mark 7) until the crumble is crisp
and golden (about 20 minutes). Serve
hot with custard or ice cream.

# Blackberry vodka

Approximate preparation time: 15 minutes, plus regular shaking and storage time

400g (14oz) blackberries

100g (3½oz) sugar

10 unpeeled almonds

1 litre (35fl oz / 1¾ pints) vodka

**1**  Two-thirds fill a bottle with blackberries.

**2**  Pour the sugar over the top.

**3**  Bruise the almonds with a rolling pin
and add them to the bottle.

**4**  Pour in the vodka to the top and
seal. Shake daily for 1 week then store
in a cool dark place for 3 months.

**5**  Strain off the liquid into another
bottle. Seal tightly and store for 1 year
before drinking.

# Bracken
## (*Pteridium aquilinum*)

The young bracken fronds are known as fiddleheads due to their resemblance to the curled scroll at the top of a violin. They have been eaten as a foodstuff in many parts of the world, and are still widely eaten today in Japan and Korea. The rhizome is consumed by Native Americans and the Māori people of New Zealand, and used to be considered a delicacy by the people of Canada. In parts of Russia the roots were fermented with barley to make a kind of beer.

## Appearance and habitat

Bracken is an extremely vigorous widespread fern, whose range extends across most of the northern hemisphere, as well as Australia, New Zealand and part of South America. It is very invasive and secretes chemicals that inhibit the growth of other plants. It is a herbaceous perennial plant with large, roughly triangular fronds growing from an underground rhizome. A bracken plant can spread from underground buds at a rate of around 1m (3') per annum. In favourable conditions it can grow as much as 3m (10') tall. The fronds turn an attractive rusty brown in autumn before dying back for the winter.

## Control

Bracken can be controlled by the use of deep mulches or by repeatedly cutting it down, although it may take 2-3 years to have a significant effect. Spot treatment with a glyphosate-based weedkiller can be effective.

## Uses

Due to the potentially carcinogenic effects, eating bracken on more than an occasional basis is not recommended (see box, right), and I do not eat it. If you do want to try the fiddleheads, though, you should first blanch them in a large saucepan of boiling, salted water for 5 minutes. Drain off the water and return them to the pan with fresh water and boil for a further 10 minutes before eating or adding to soups, rice dishes or frying with onions and soy sauce.

Bracken can be used in horticulture as a mulching agent and in the manufacture of composts. It is also used in place of straw in chicken houses or as bedding for animals, but should be used with the same reservations as for human consumption if the animals are likely to eat it. The ash resulting from burning bracken was at one time collected, processed with oil, and made into balls as a form of soap.

## Related plants

The fiddleheads of ostrich fern are considered a traditional dish in parts of New England in the USA and in some regions of Canada. The Asian fern species known as vegetable fern is widely eaten in stir-fries in countries such as the Philippines and Thailand.

❶ **CAUTION: Eating bracken has been associated with an increased incidence of oesophageal and stomach cancers in Japan.[2] It contains a carcinogen called ptaquiloside, which has been found in the milk of cows that feed on bracken, and even in water supplies in areas where bracken grows in profusion.[3] Many ferns also contain the enzyme thiaminase, which breaks down thiamine (vitamin B1), and regular consumption of large quantities can result in the vitamin deficiency disease known as beriberi. The fiddleheads of ostrich fern have been associated with a number of cases of gastrointestinal illnesses, particularly when eaten raw or undercooked.**

# Brooklime
## (*Veronica beccabunga*)

Brooklime has been widely used as a salad plant in northern Europe. In the seventeenth century it developed the reputation as an antiscorbutic herb, being promoted for the condition known as land scurvy. Because of this it is often said even today to be extremely high in vitamin C, despite evidence showing that this is not in fact the case.[4] While brooklime may not be as beneficial as was widely believed, it does contain more vitamin C than most cultivated lettuces, and so can be a useful addition to a salad. It has a bitter taste that seems to be less acceptable to modern tastebuds than it was formerly.

## Appearance and habitat

Related to the speedwells, which often colonise lawns, brooklime (as its common name indicates) prefers to grow by brooks and streams or in damp ground. Also known as water pimpernel or cow cress, it is a member of the plantain family (Plantaginaceae), along with plantains and foxgloves. It forms a dense sprawling mass of succulent, oblong, dark green leaves which are virtually evergreen. It flowers from late spring throughout the summer. The small, deep-blue flowers with white eyes are carried in profusion on the upper parts of the stems. The small blue brooklime leaf beetle, perhaps unsurprisingly given its name, feeds solely on the leaves of this plant.

## Uses

The leaves can be eaten raw or cooked. They have a very tart taste and can add an interesting pungency to a mix of other salad leaves. If you prefer milder flavours, try soaking the leaves in salt water for half an hour before rinsing and boiling them until wilted. They can then be used as you would spinach.

## Related species

The American speedwell, *Veronica americana*, is similar to brooklime and can be eaten in the same way, but sadly most of the other common speedwells have an unpleasant taste.

**CAUTION: Be sure that you identify the plant correctly. It has been confused with the very poisonous dog's mercury (*Mercurialis perennis*); see warning regarding the latter species on page 47.**

**As with watercress, wild brooklime must not be eaten raw if there is a chance that it could be contaminated with larvae of the liver fluke. This parasitic flatworm has a life cycle that involves pond snails and commonly infects cows and sheep that graze on marshy pastures. Cooking kills all stages of the fluke.**

## Brooklime and ricotta lasagne

Serves 4
Approximate preparation time: 1 hour

50g (1¾oz) butter
50g (1¾oz) plain flour
570ml (20fl oz / 1 pint) milk
50g (1¾oz) Parmesan cheese, grated
400g (14oz) brooklime
400g (14oz) ricotta
12 sheets fresh lasagne

1  Make a white sauce with the butter, flour and milk.

2  Once it has thickened, stir in the Parmesan cheese.

3  Wash the brooklime carefully and boil for a minute or so until wilted, then drain thoroughly in a colander.

4  Cream the ricotta then layer with the pasta and brooklime in a lasagne dish. Finish with the white sauce and cook in a medium oven (180°C / 350°F / Gas Mark 4) for about 30 minutes till golden.

# Burdock
## (*Arctium lappa*)

A plant of roadsides and scrubby land, burdock is probably best known for its use in the soft drink dandelion and burdock. However, its other significant claim to fame is as the inspiration for Velcro® fastening, invented in 1941 by the Swiss engineer Georges de Mestral, who was intrigued by the way the burrs of burdock stuck firmly to his clothes and to the fur of his dog.

The burrs themselves play a starring role in the bizarre Burry Man parade, which is held in August each year in South Queensferry, near Edinburgh. A man, uncomfortably decorated from head to foot in some 11,000 burrs, walks around the streets from 9am to 6pm, guided by two attendants. The custom is said to have originated as a way of bringing luck to the local fishermen in the hope that fish would stick to their nets as burrs stick to the man.

The large leaves were used in the days before refrigerators to wrap butter, as with the leaves of butterbur.

## Appearance and habitat

The capacity of burrs to allow seeds to be carried long distances by animals – and indeed by humans – means that although burdock is native to temperate regions of Europe, Africa and Asia, it has naturalised almost everywhere. Burdock is a biennial plant, related to thistles, in the daisy family (Compositae). It has matt green leaves that are white underneath. In good growing conditions the leaves can reach dramatic proportions.

Burdock flowers from July to September, and the burrs are present even when flowers are in bud. The purplish flowers, held within balls of hooks, are carried on branched stems that can

reach 1.5-2m (5'-6'6") in height. The flowers are popular with bees, butterflies and hoverflies.

## Uses

The leaves of burdock are said to be edible and are sometimes recommended for use in place of vine leaves in dishes such as dolmas. They are, however, quite bitter, and few people find them palatable. Sushi eaters may have tried *hotategai*, a kind of scallop that may be served wrapped in burdock leaf. In late spring the young flowering stems can be cut and peeled, then boiled for 5-10 minutes in a small quantity of water. They are eaten like asparagus with melted butter.

However, it is the roots that are most widely used as a vegetable. They were commonly eaten throughout Europe in the Middle Ages, and remain popular today in Japan, where they are called *gobo*. Harvest the roots before the plant sends up its flowering stem, as the older roots become bitter. Cut them into short lengths, peel and soak in water for 10 minutes before draining and cooking. They can be boiled and served as a side dish or used in

CAUTION: The cooked root is low in fat but high in dietary fibre, containing the polysaccharide inulin, which can be somewhat difficult to digest.

stir-fries. They are crunchy, with a texture something like bamboo shoots, and have a sweet, earthy flavour. The roots can also be scrubbed, then wrapped in foil and roasted on a barbecue or in the hot ashes of a fire. They take up to an hour to soften, when they can be served with a knob of butter or a splash of soy sauce.

Dandelion and burdock is traditionally made from the fermented roots of dandelion and burdock plants, but many modern drinks sold under the name are actually just carbonated soft drinks with artificial flavourings. There is still one manufacturer in Britain who produces a traditionally fermented version, described as 'botanically brewed', which has added ginger and aniseed flavours. Unfortunately, the aniseed flavour tends to dominate. There has been a recent revival of interest in the drink, and recipes for dandelion and burdock cakes made with it feature on many websites.

Variations on the dandelion and burdock drink are made with scrubbed burdock roots and either roots, leaves or even the flowers of dandelions. The dandelions give quite a bitter taste, so use a larger proportion of burdock if you have a sweet tooth. Fermented versions were traditionally bottled in stone jars, but even these could explode under the pressure of the fermentation. For safety use plastic rather than glass bottles, and use a fermenter with an airlock, or cover with cling film pierced with a pinhole to allow the gas to escape.

## Related species

Lesser burdock, *Arctium minus*, is a very similar species with smaller flowers that have shorter stalks than those of *A. lappa*. Most thistles have also been used as food but you need stout gloves to gather the young shoots and strip them of spines. The flowerheads of any of them can be treated as miniature globe artichokes but are very fiddly to deal with.

**CAUTION: Thistles have deep taproots and can accumulate toxic amounts of nitrates, so it is sensible not to eat any growing on land that is regularly treated with fertiliser.**

## Dandelion and burdock beer

Approximate preparation time: 2 hours, plus time to ferment

Root of 1 large dandelion
Roots of 1-2 burdocks
4 litres (140fl oz / 7 pints water
400g (14oz) sugar
2 tbsp black treacle
Juice and zest of 1 lemon
30g (1oz) yeast

**1** Scrub the roots and bash them with a rolling pin.

**2** Put in a large pan with 2 litres (70fl oz / 3½ pints) water and boil for 30 minutes.

**3** Strain the liquid and discard the roots.

**4** Return the liquid to the pan and stir in the sugar, treacle, juice and lemon zest. Heat until the sugar has dissolved.

**5** Pour liquid into a brewer's bucket and add another 2 litres (70fl oz / 3½ pints) of water. The mix should be about blood temperature.

**6** Sprinkle with the yeast, insert airlock or cover with pierced cling film, and leave to ferment for 3-4 days before bottling. Drink after 1 week; its keeping qualities will depend upon the amount of alcohol produced. The alcohol level is variable, so be wary if you are planning on driving afterwards.

# Campion
## (*Silene* spp.)

The scientific name *Silene* comes from Silenus, the wise, but usually drunken, companion of the Greek wine-god Dionysus, which may perhaps explain the tendency of *Silene latifolia* to sprawl all over its companion plants.

Campions belong to a group of plants that can be considered either as wildflowers or as weeds, depending on your point of view. They are attractive herbaceous perennials with pretty flowers that attract bees and night-flying moths. However, they do seed them-selves around with great abandon and the deep roots can be difficult to remove, especially on clay soils. The young leaves of S. *vulgaris* are particu-larly rich in vitamin C, containing an average of 27mg per 100g, nearly three times that of cos lettuce.

## Appearance and habitat

Red campion, *Silene dioica*, also known by the country name of Robin Hood, is widely distributed in decidu-ous woodlands and in hedgerows on fertile, limy soils. It flowers in early summer, with the rosy-red flowers being pollinated by long-tongued bees and flies. It is a perennial plant, growing up to around 1m (3') tall.

White campion, S. *latifolia*, is a weed of arable land and waste areas, growing well on dry soils. It is an annual or short-lived perennial, flowering throughout the summer. It can be taller than the red species but often flops on the ground.

The flowers are slightly clove-scented at night and attract moths. Plants are resistant to mowing and will regrow from the root if the top growth is pulled off or burned. Red campion generally grows in moister conditions than white campion, but where they grow together they can produce pink-flowered fertile hybrids. The bladder campion, *S. vulgaris*, is a plant of arable fields, hedgerows and roadsides, flourishing on disturbed ground, especially on limy soils. Its common name derives from the bladder-like calyx of the flower, which can be 'popped' like a fuchsia flower before the flowers have opened.

Campions are in the family Caryophyllaceae and are related to chickweeds, garden pinks and soapwort (also known as Bouncing Bet). Like soapwort, all campions contain saponins (see page 52). The level of saponins in a plant can vary; red campion tends to have higher levels than white or bladder campions, and this is indicated by the more bitter taste of the leaves. Saponin levels are usually reduced by soaking in water and cooking.

Flowers of red, white and pink campions.

## Uses

The flowers of any campion species can be used to add interest to salads. The young leaves of red, white and bladder campions are used in spring stews in the Veneto and Val Colvera areas of northern Italy.

Bladder campion is eaten as a green vegetable in several European countries. In Spain, where the plant is known as *colleja*, the young shoots and leaves are eaten raw in salads and the older leaves are sautéed with garlic, and used in omelettes or with rice. Plants growing in the shade of taller shrubs and trees are usually more tender than those growing in full sun.

Not to be confused with the cold vegetable-based soups of Andalucía, *gazpacho manchego* is a meat stew from the Spanish region of La Mancha, usually made with rabbit and a flatbread referred to as a *torta de gazpacho*. The Spanish dish known as *gazpachos viudos*, or 'widow's gazpacho', traditionally uses *collejas* instead of meat, although today spinach is often substituted for the *collejas*. The name implies that an essential ingredient is missing, the meat being equated with the husband.

## Related plants

*Saponaria officinalis* (soapwort, or Bouncing Bet) is still used as a shampoo and for washing delicate fabrics. During summer cut the leaves, stems and flowers. Boil 1 cup of chopped plant with 2 cups of water for 20-30 minutes, then use the resulting liquid as soap. The roots can be lifted and dried for use in winter, when 1 tablespoon of chopped dried root is used per cup of water.

Soapwort is a robust garden plant.

## Spanish chickpeas and collejas

Serves 4
Approximate preparation time: 45 minutes

1 large Spanish onion, chopped

1 tbsp olive oil

1 large potato, weight about 300g (10½oz), peeled and diced

100g (3½oz) cooked gammon or thick-cut ham, diced

1 green pepper, diced

1 beefsteak tomato, diced

1 tbsp paprika

1 cup chicken or vegetable stock

400g (14oz) can chickpeas (garbanzo beans) (or use dried chickpeas soaked overnight and boiled 1-2 hours until soft)

2 generous handfuls of *collejas* (bladder campion), young shoots and leaves

**1** Fry the onion in the olive oil.

**2** Add the potato to the pan with the onion, stirring from time to time to prevent sticking.

**3** Add the gammon, pepper and tomato to the pan with the paprika and stock. Stir, cover, then allow to simmer gently for about 30 minutes until the potato is soft.

**4** Add the drained and rinsed chickpeas, then the *collejas*. Cook for a further minute or so and then serve with crusty bread or focaccia.

## Summer berry salad recipe

Serves 4
Approximate preparation time: 1-2 hours (including marinating time)

400g (14oz) strawberries, halved
200g (7oz) raspberries or loganberries
200g (7oz) blueberries
2 tbsp orange juice
1 tbsp demerara sugar
1 tbsp Pimms®
Handful of campion flowers

**1**  Mix the fruit together in a bowl.

**2**  Heat the orange juice and sugar together until boiling. Turn off the heat and stir in the Pimms®.

**3**  Pour the liquid over the berries and leave to marinate for an hour or so. Scatter the flowers over the fruit and serve with whipped cream and lavender shortbread biscuits.


## Widow's gazpacho

Serves 4
Approximate preparation time: 30 minutes

1 large potato, chopped
4 cloves garlic, chopped
4 tomatoes, chopped
4 tbsp olive oil
2 cups water or vegetable stock
1 *torta de gazpacho* (or substitute flatbread)
200-300g (7-10½oz) *collejas* (bladder campion)
Ground black pepper

**1**  Fry the potato, garlic and tomatoes in the olive oil.

**2**  Add the water or stock and simmer for 10-15 minutes.

**3**  Tear or cut the *torta* into bite-sized pieces and add to the pan. Cook for a further 10 minutes until soft.

**4**  Add the *collejas* and cook for another couple of minutes; season with pepper, and serve.

# Chickweed
## (*Stellaria media*)

In Victorian times, when the keeping of caged birds was popular, many people scraped a living by selling chickweed and groundsel at one halfpenny a bunch in London.[5] The famous painting *Work* by Ford Madox Brown is said to feature a chickweed seller, although his basket seems to feature forget-me-nots. Chickweed is also of benefit in the human diet as it contains several essential minerals, including magnesium.

## Appearance and habitat

Chickweed is probably the most common and familiar of annual weeds, particularly in moist conditions. It has small, bright green oval leaves, a sprawling growth habit and starry white flowers at virtually any time of year. It seeds quickly and prolifically, completing its life cycle in as little as 5-6 weeks, but is generally easily removed by hand pulling or hoeing. The plant itself, as the common name indicates, makes a useful foodstuff for chickens and is given to cage birds.

## Uses

Chickweed is usually eaten as a salad vegetable – harvest it with a pair of kitchen scissors. The flowers, leaves and stems are all edible, though mature plants get a bit stringy. The flowers look pretty in salads, but do close up quite quickly when harvested.

Chickweed has a mild, grassy taste and is more acceptable to children than many other wild greens. It can be used like cress in egg sandwiches, or boiled briefly like spinach or added to soups, stews and sauces. Fried in butter with chopped onion, it makes a delicate-tasting green vegetable.

## Related species

Most of the other chickweeds, including greater stitchwort (*Stellaria holostea*), have higher levels of saponins, which can give them a bitter taste, so they are best avoided.

# Chicory

## (*Cichorium intybus*)

Chicory is native to Britain and Europe but has naturalised in North America and Australia. The ancient Egyptians and the Romans grew it as a vegetable, and in northern Europe it has been cultivated since at least the sixteenth century. It was widely grown for its medicinal properties and as a coffee substitute. Chicory greens contain significant quantities of vitamins A and C.

## Appearance and habitat

Chicory, also known as wild succory, is found on grasslands and waste ground on dry limy soils. It is a perennial plant in the daisy family (Asteraceae) and grows to about 1m (3') tall. It flowers from July to October with beautiful sky-blue flowers loved by bees and hoverflies. Forms with pink or white flowers are sometimes seen.

## Uses

The leaves of wild chicory are quite bitter, yet pleasing, and can be used to add a tang to salads and soups. Boiling the leaves in plenty of water reduces the bitterness and they can then be used as a green vegetable or in pasta sauces. The plants can also be blanched by forcing them under a flower pot, in a similar way to the commercial production of clusters of chicory leaves (known as chicons), to reduce the bitterness.

For use as a coffee substitute the taproots of first-year plants are roasted until crisp, then ground. It is very bitter, so is usually mixed with coffee.

CAUTION: As with several other members of the daisy family, such as Jerusalem artichokes, the roots of chicory contain large quantities of the storage polysaccharide inulin, which can cause bloating and discomfort if eaten in quantity.

# Clover
## (*Trifolium* spp.)

White clover, *Trifolium repens*, is a widespread and familiar plant, also known affectionately as bee-bread or sheepy-maa's. Clover has a high protein content and is a very valuable forage plant for grazing animals and poultry. The flowers are rich in nectar and the pollen high in protein. The Pomo tribes of North America thought so highly of clover as a crop that special clover feasts were held in early spring.

## Appearance and habitat

There are some 250 species of clover, of which the white or Dutch clover, *Trifolium repens*, is probably the best known. Each leaf is composed of three leaflets held in the characteristic trefoil shape. The variants with four leaves have long been considered to be lucky, but the record for the greatest number of leaflets goes to Shigeo Obara of Japan, who in May 2009 found one with 56 leaflets.[6] The leaves often have white chevron markings on them.

White clover has creeping stems that root at the nodes, and forms large, spreading patches in lawns, meadows and at roadsides. It is a common lawn weed as it is tolerant of mowing and trampling. The rounded flowerheads contain between 40 and 100 individual white flowers, which age to brown.

Red clover, *T. pratense*, is another common species, although it is usually less invasive in the garden. It has several cultivated forms that are grown as fodder crops and are widely natural-ised in the Americas and in Australasia.

## Uses

The leaves are edible and have a mild pea-like flavour, but are fairly chewy and indigestible, even when cooked. If eaten to excess they can cause bloating. The flowers have a rich, sweet scent and can be eaten scattered over salads or dried to use in herbal teas. They can also be used to make a delightful clover blossom syrup, a lovely amber-coloured liquid – like bottled summer! It can be used as a honey substitute.

Herbalists often recommend red clover as a cure for menopausal problems as it contains oestrogen-like compounds, but a controlled study did not show major benefits when compared with placebos.[7] It should not be eaten in large quantities due to the alkaloid content.

**CAUTION: Be wary of using the alsike clover, *T. hybridum*, as it has caused toxicity in horses, producing a photosensitivity known as trifoliosis (dew poisoning) and irreversible liver disease. The specific toxin has not been identified, but is thought to come from a fungus which infects the plant. It is more likely to be a problem in conditions of high rainfall and humidity.**

## Clover blossom syrup

Approximate preparation time: 1 hour, plus time to infuse

2 large mugfuls clover flowers
Half an unpeeled orange, chopped
1 litre (35fl oz / 1¾ pints) water
1kg (2lb 3oz) sugar

**1** Put the flowers and fruit into a large pan with the water and bring to the boil.

**2** Turn off the heat, cover the pan and leave to infuse overnight.

**3** Strain through muslin or a tea towel, squeezing all the liquid out.

**4** Return the liquid to the rinsed pan. Add the sugar to the liquid, then slowly bring to the boil, stirring now and then.

**5** Simmer until the liquid has reduced to a thick syrup.

**6** Bottle in sterile jars, and seal. The sugar may start to crystallise out fairly quickly, but the syrup tastes so good it does not usually last long anyway.

# Comfrey
## (*Symphytum* spp.)

Comfrey was probably first introduced to Britain as a fodder crop, but is widely naturalised. The common name, knitbone, refers to its use in herbal medicine. Roots were lifted in spring and grated to make a poultice to aid healing. Comfrey is unusual among plants in that it is a source of vitamin B12. However, you would have to eat at least 1.8kg (4lb) of the leaves in order to obtain your daily requirement of the vitamin, and this would not be recommended due to the level of alkaloids in the leaves.

## Appearance and habitat

The name 'comfrey' is used for several closely related species and the hybrids between them. The common comfrey, *Symphytum officinale*, is a perennial plant growing to some 1.2m (4'). It has bristly leaves and bell-like flowers of pale cream or purple that hang in clusters in May and June.

White comfrey, *S. orientale*, is native to Turkey and western Russia but is now widely naturalised elsewhere. Its pure white flowers normally open a couple of weeks earlier than those of the common comfrey.

Russian comfrey, *S. × uplandicum*, is a purplish-flowered hybrid between *S. officinale* and *S. asperum*, the rough comfrey.

## Uses

Comfrey has long-established uses for medicinal and culinary purposes. In the past young shoots and leaves were eaten in salads and as a boiled vegetable. The roots have been used

Making comfrey fertiliser.

Green alkanet.

for wine, and in Germany fritters are made from the leaves.

Comfrey is also a valuable plant for organic gardeners, as the deep roots draw up minerals from the subsoil and the plant can be used to make a high-quality plant fertiliser. Fill a bucket with comfrey, top up with water, cover it and leave in an unregarded corner of the garden until it goes brown and smelly. Pour off the liquid and use as a high-potassium feed for tomatoes and other fruit crops. If the liquid turns out very thick and dark, use diluted with water. A cultivar of Russian comfrey, 'Bocking 14' is often planted for this purpose as it is sterile and so will not seed itself. It was developed in the 1950s by Lawrence Hills, the founder of the Henry Doubleday Research Association, now known as Garden Organic.

## Related plants

Green alkanet (*Pentaglottis sempervirens*), which comes from south-west Europe, looks like a particularly robust forget-me-not, with bristly leaves and bright blue flowers in May and June. The flowers are pretty and the plant may be tolerated in shady situations, but it has deep fleshy roots which can be difficult to remove and a tendency to seed itself madly. Pull up the top growth and use it like comfrey to make an organic plant food.

**CAUTION: It is important to be aware of the potential risks of ingesting comfrey. It contains pyrrolizidine alkaloids, with higher levels present in the young leaves. These could cause liver damage if consumed regularly or in large quantities. Species such as *Symphytum asperum* can accumulate nitrates from the soil, from which toxic nitrites are formed. Handling the plant can cause skin irritation.**

**It is safest to restrict comfrey use to the topical applications of poultices for healing wounds.**

# Common bistort
## (*Persicaria bistorta*)

Bistort has a long history of use in a springtime dish made from cooked wild greens with oatmeal. Traditionally eaten in the two weeks before Easter, it is a bitter dish considered suitable to cleanse the system and replenish supplies of vitamins and other nutrients after the winter. Bistort itself is variously called Easter ledger, Easterman giants, pudding dock and passion dock. The World Dock Pudding Championship is an annual event in Yorkshire, held in an attempt to maintain interest in this local custom. Competitors use their own variations of the basic ingredients of pudding dock, nettles, onions and oatmeal, fried in bacon fat. The puddings are cooked in front of an audience to the tune of the local brass band.

## Appearance and habitat

Common bistort, a member of the family Polygonaceae, has large arrow- or heart-shaped, stalked leaves that can look silvery beneath. The unbranched stems, reaching up to 70cm (2'4"), carry spikes of pink flowers from May to August. It is a plant of wet meadows, ditches and alder carr (areas of damp meadow favourable to alder). In Britain it is found most frequently in north-west England, where it is usually known as pudding dock.

## Uses

The leaves can be eaten raw but are somewhat tough, so are better cooked. Young leaves, harvested before the plant comes into flower, have the better taste. Cooking will tend to lessen the bitterness of the leaves. The roots can be also eaten, as you would water chestnuts.

The plentiful seeds can be eaten whole, incorporated into cakes and flapjacks or ground into flour, but are rather fiddly to collect.

## Related plants

The leaves, young shoots and roots of various other species of *Persicaria* and the closely related polygonums are sometimes used as foods in different cultures. The leaves of *Persicaria chinensis*, known locally as *ameta*, are used as a vegetable by the people of West Bengal. The cylindrical flower spikes of species such as red bistort (*P. amplexicaule*) are very attractive and so the plants are often grown for ornamental purposes, although they may be somewhat invasive. If you have an excess of the plant, you could do as the people of Pakistan do: locally the root of *P. amplexicaule* is mixed with egg and fried in cow's ghee, as a general body tonic.

Alpine bistort (*P. vivipara*) produces

Red bistort has striking flowers.

tiny bulbils along the lower part of the flower stalks. These can be removed and eaten raw.

**CAUTION: RELATED PLANTS. You should exercise a certain amount of caution with the other *Persicaria* species, as some have an acrid sap which can act as a skin irritant or stimulate photosensitisation of the skin.**

## Dock pudding

Serves 4
Approximate preparation time: 30 minutes

400g (14oz) pudding dock leaves

200g (7oz) young nettle tops

A few blackcurrant leaves if available

2 large onions, chopped (or 2 handfuls of wild garlic leaves)

Knob of butter or bacon fat to fry

Handful of oatmeal

1  Thoroughly wash the dock leaves and nettles, removing any stalks.

2  Fry with onions until soft.

3  Add the oatmeal and cook for 15-20 minutes, stirring to prevent sticking. Serve with rashers of bacon.

# Common mallow
## (*Malva sylvestris*)

The first synthetic dye (aniline purple), synthesised in 1856 by William Perkin, an 18-year-old chemistry student, was named mauveine after the purple flowers of *Malva*. Mallow leaves have a higher content of polyunsaturated fatty acids than those of many cultivated vegetables and are a good source of vitamin C.

## Appearance and habitat

A widespread perennial plant often growing on verges and waste ground, mallow can grow to around 1.5m (5') tall but more often prefers to sprawl across the ground. In the warmer climate of North Africa it usually grows as an annual plant. The crinkly leaves have a tendency to attract dust and can become infected with a rusty-coloured fungus (*Puccinia malvacearum*). The flowers are mauve-pink with darker stripes and can be seen at any time from April through to the autumn. They are pollinated by bees. Plants from the genus *Malva* are food for the larvae of the painted lady butterfly.

There are various ornamental selections cultivated in gardens including 'Zebrina', which has particularly attractive pale flowers striped in a deep purple-black. After flowering the developing seedpods form little nutlets. They were known as pick-cheeses by country children and were eaten as a small, slightly nutty-tasting snack food.

## Uses

Mallow and similar species such as melokhia are included in many Middle Eastern dishes, especially in soups, where they act as a thickener. They have been a staple food in Egypt since the time of the pharaohs and are portrayed in ancient tomb paintings. They were often served in soup or mixed with meats and other vegetables.

The leaves of mallow can be eaten raw in salads but do not have any great taste and are probably better incorporated into cooked dishes. Dip the leaves in tempura batter and deep fry in olive oil for an interesting snack. Once cooked, the leaves are somewhat mucilaginous, like okra, which is in the same family. The leaves may be dried for winter use.

The flowers make an attractive addition to salads or a garnish for desserts.

The unripe seedpods can be gathered and nibbled on while out walking, or added to salads and stews.

The fibrous stems of mallow are used in paper making. The plant can also be used as a natural yellow dye.

## Related plants

The annual *Malva verticillata* is useful for inclusion in leafy salads. The leaves do tend to wilt quickly, so they are best picked just before preparing the salad. An attractive curled-leaf form in cultivation, *M. verticillata* 'Crispa', will self-seed like the wild species.

The marsh mallow, *Althaea officinalis*, is a tall perennial up to 2m (6'6") high with soft, grey, woolly leaves and pale lilac-pink flowers. It grows in damp habitats such as salty marshes, ditches and beside streams. The roots have been used to make marshmallow sweets since ancient Egyptian times. Both roots and stems contain sufficient gelatinous material to be turned into jelly when infused in water. Modern marshmallows, however, are made with corn syrup, water and gelatine. The dried roots are known in France as *hochets de guimauves* and are sold as teethers for babies and as a herbal remedy for coughs and sore throats.

Other plants in the Malvaceae family are in great demand for their fibres, which are known as jute.

### Egyptian khubayza stew

Serves 4
Approximate preparation time: 1 hour 30 minutes

400g (14oz) mallow or melokhia leaves

30g (1oz) butter

1 large onion, chopped

4 cloves garlic

200g (7oz) lean lamb, diced

1 litre (35fl oz / 1¾ pints) meat stock

1 tin chickpeas

1 bunch fresh coriander, chopped

**1** Fry the mallow leaves in the butter until wilted, then remove from pan and set aside.

**2** Gently fry the onion and garlic until they are starting to colour then add the meat and stir for a few minutes.

**3** Pour in the stock and simmer for about an hour until the meat is tender.

**4** Add the mallow leaves and drained chickpeas and cook for a further 10-15 minutes.

**5** Add the coriander before serving with couscous or flatbreads.

# Dandelion
## (*Taraxacum officinale* agg.)

The name 'dandelion' comes from the French *dents-de-lion*, meaning lion's teeth, referring to the golden petals. The seedheads are used by children as clocks to tell the time – the number of puffs needed to blow away all the seeds gives the hour. Catching a feathery plume with its seed still attached entitles you to make a wish. Dandelion seeds spread further in hot weather as the seeds are carried higher in the air. Some have been shown to have travelled more than 1km (¾ mile), although the vast majority will land less than 10m (33') from the parent plant. Dandelion leaves are a rich source of several vitamins including vitamins A, C, E and K and some of the B vitamins. They also provide useful amounts of iron and other minerals.

## Appearance and habitat

Botanists like to make life complicated and use *Taraxacum officinale* as an aggregate name to cover more than 200 'micro-species' in Britain alone. From a culinary point of view, though, a dandelion is a dandelion and all of them are edible. With their golden, shaggy flowerheads that turn to spheres of silver seeds and the rosettes of jagged leaves, dandelions are plants that everyone can recognise. Individual dandelion plants, treasured in a cottage garden, can live for 25 years or more and develop into very attractive specimen plants which will produce hundreds of flowers.

## Uses

Dandelions have probably been used for both culinary and medicinal purposes for thousands of years. The genus name is derived from the Greek words *taraxos*, meaning 'disorder', and *akos*, for 'remedy'. They have been used in folk remedies in many cultures around the world. The roots in particular can have a diuretic effect, which explains the alternative French name for them of *pissenlits* (wet-the-bed).

The common dandelion is a biennial or perennial plant with a sturdy taproot that can reach depths of 1m (3') or more. It can produce seed without pollination, resulting in offspring which are genetically identical to the parent.

In Britain dandelion leaves were traditionally harvested before St George's Day on 23rd April, when they are likely to be more tender and less bitter. The season can be extended by blanching the dandelions, which reduces the bitterness. To do this they can be earthed up by mounding soil up over them as is done with leeks; or, more simply, placing a plate or upturning a bucket over them for a few days.

In France dandelions are still widely cultivated as a green vegetable and they can often be found for sale on market stalls. Different cultivars have been selected over time, which are naturally less bitter or at least easier to blanch. 'Amélioré à Coeur Plein' has a clumping growth habit with the leaves held tightly together so it tends to blanch itself naturally. 'Vert de Montmogny', named for the commune

Dandelion leaves go well in salad.

in Val-d'Oise, is an early-maturing cultivar. It has broad, dark green leaves, which are quite mild without blanching. 'Arlington' resembles a chicory and is larger and milder than the wild dandelion. The Italian dandelion 'Italiko Rossa' is a particularly attractive plant with deep maroon-red stems and midribs to the leaves.

The leaves are used raw in salads and sandwiches. They go well with salted meats such as ham or bacon. If you find them too bitter raw, try them lightly fried in butter for a minute or two or combined with a bacon dressing in the traditional French dish *pissenlits au lard*.

Roots are best dug in the autumn, when they are at their fattest, and can be baked until brittle, then ground into a caffeine-free coffee substitute. Alternatively, they can be cooked as a root vegetable by first blanching in water then frying in butter for a few minutes before adding a little water or stock and simmering gently until tender. They are also used in the classic British soft drink dandelion and burdock.

The flowers can be used to make a blossom syrup that is a speciality of the Franche Comté region of France, where it is known as *cremaillotte*. It is traditionally made with 365 flowers, one for each day of the year. It is a fairly laborious process as all the green bitter parts of the flower should be removed. This is easiest to do in the middle of the day, when the flowers are wide open; if you leave it until the evening you will find that the flowers have closed. The same will apply if you are picking the flowers to make dandelion wine or to dip them in batter for flower fritters.

## Related species

*Taraxacum kok-saghyz*, the Russian or rubber dandelion, was used in several countries during the Second World War as a source of rubber when supplies of tropical rubber were impossible to obtain. It can also be used as a source of the polysaccharide inulin, which can be turned into bioethanol by fermentation.

## Dandelion beer

Approximate preparation time: 2 hours plus time to ferment

200g (7oz) dandelion roots
15g (½oz) ginger root
Rind and juice of 1 lemon
4.5 litres (160fl oz / 8 pints) water
400g (14oz) demerara sugar
30g (1oz) cream of tartar
30g (1oz) brewer's yeast

1  Wash and remove any small fibrous roots from the dandelions, retaining the thick taproots.

2  Bruise the ginger and put with the dandelions and lemon rind in the water; boil for 20 minutes.

3  Strain on to the sugar, lemon juice and cream of tartar and stir to dissolve.

4  Allow to cool to about 20°C (70°F), add the yeast and cover. Allow to ferment in a warm place for 3 days.

5  Bottle in screw-top bottles. Test daily to ensure it does not get too fizzy, so that the bottles do not explode.

## Cremaillotte

Approximate preparation time: 1 hour, plus time to infuse

1 lemon, chopped

1 orange, chopped

365 dandelions (green parts removed)

1 litre (35fl oz / 1¾ pints) water

Sugar

**1** Put the lemon and orange in a pan with the washed dandelions and water.

**2** Boil gently for 10 minutes then leave to infuse overnight.

**3** Strain through muslin and add 1kg (2lb 3oz) of sugar for every 50ml (nearly 2fl oz) of liquid produced.

**4** Bring to the boil and simmer for 10 minutes then bottle in sterile glass jars, and seal.

## Pissenlits au lard

Serves about 4
Approximate preparation time: 15 minutes

400g (14oz) young fresh dandelion leaves (or mix half-and-half with baby spinach leaves)

6 thick rashers streaky bacon, cut into strips

1 tsp walnut or olive oil

*For the dressing:*

4 tbsp olive oil

1 tbsp white wine vinegar

Pinch of sugar

Ground black pepper

**1** Make the dressing first, by shaking all the ingredients together in a stoppered bottle.

**2** Wash the dandelion leaves and shake dry.

**3** Fry the bacon in the oil.

**4** Put the leaves in a bowl and add the salad dressing lightly. When the bacon is crisp and brown, pour it – with all its fat – over the salad, and serve immediately.

# Dittander
## (*Lepidium latifolium*)

Dittander is also commonly known as pepperweed, due to the hot peppery taste of the leaves. It is valued in many parts of the world for its nutritious leaves, which can be grown even at high altitude regions such as Ladakh in northern India.

## Appearance and habitat

Dittander is a perennial plant that spreads by rhizomes to form quite large colonies. It has large elegant oval leaves up to 30cm (1') long. They are somewhat leathery in texture and of an attractive greyish-green colour with lightly toothed edges. The tiny white flowers are held in loose, airy clusters in midsummer. It is a member of the large cabbage family, but is not easily confused with its relatives.

In Britain it is found mostly around the east and south coasts, but it also spreads along railway tracks. It is said to be a nationally scarce species, but in the garden it is extremely competitive and can be invasive. In former times it was used as a herbal remedy for leprosy, and colonies still exist around the sites of former leper hospitals.

## Uses

The roots of dittander have a hot, pungent taste and it was widely used as a condiment before the introduction of horseradish.

The leaves have a very hot, cress-like taste when eaten raw, but this is mostly lost when they are cooked. The finely chopped leaves can be added to Hollandaise sauce or gravies to serve with beef. Alternatively, use them to make a fiery-flavoured pesto for pasta or to spread in cold meat sandwiches.

Dittander is also known as poor man's pepper, and the fresh, green seeds have a hot, spicy flavour. The volatile oils which give the plant its flavour are soon lost, however, so it is not worth saving the seeds for any length of time.

# Dock
## (*Rumex* spp.)

Docks are familiar and widespread weeds. Most dock species have leaves that are high in vitamins such as B1 (thiamine) and vitamin C. They are edible in small quantities but you should restrict portion sizes due to the high oxalic acid content. The curled dock (*Rumex crispus*) is a useful source of omega-3 fatty acids, containing 34mg per 100g of raw leaves. All docks provide small amounts of iron and zinc.

## Appearance and habitat

There are many species of dock and they hybridise freely so can be difficult to identify. Curled dock (*Rumex crispus*) is one of the most widely distributed plants in the world. It is found on wasteland, road verges, hedgerows and gardens and is a serious pest of agricultural land. It is a tall, perennial plant growing to around 1m (3') and is identified by the parallel-sided leaves which have a wavy margin. Broad-leaved dock (*R. obtusifolius*) has wider leaves. Both flower from June to October and are wind-pollinated. Some plants flower twice a year.

In the UK these two species are included in the list of five plants scheduled as injurious weeds under the Weeds Act 1959.

Patience dock (*R. patientia*), some-times called herb patience, is a robust species with broad leaves growing to 2m (6'6") tall. It normally flowers in May and June and was formerly cultivated as a vegetable, providing valuable greens early in the season. A fresh supply of tender leaves are often produced in the autumn. Sorrels, such as the common sorrel (*R. acetosa*), are distinguished from docks by their spear-shaped leaves with two down-ward-pointing lobes at the base, and by the sharp acid taste. Herb suppliers sometimes sell seeds of red-veined sorrel. This is thought to be a form of the wood dock (*R. sanguineus*) but red-veined sorrel presumably sounds more appetising than the alternative common name of bloody dock. The leaves do not have the lobes of sorrel leaves but are distinguished by the dramatic red veins. The baby leaves of this plant look really appealing in salads.

## Uses

The leaves of docks are frequently used as a remedy for nettle stings but are rarely used nowadays as a source of food, despite the fact that species such as the patience dock were originally introduced to many countries as a pot-herb. Patience dock is also sometimes known as monk's rhubarb as it was often grown in monastery gardens and the stalks were used as rhubarb. It is still valued as a leaf vegetable in Eastern Europe and is sold by some herb nurseries in Britain. It has a pleasant, tangy taste. Bloody dock is very similar in taste but more attractive due to the beautiful red veins.

Other docks mostly have quite a sour flavour, which is not usually acceptable to modern tastebuds. Leaves can be sliced into ribbons and used sparingly in green salads. As they are naturally sour you do not need a vinegar-based salad dressing. Cooked leaves have a mucilaginous texture and can be used to thicken soups and stews. It is likely, though, that the coarser docks would be eaten only out of dire necessity rather than for pleasure.

**CAUTION: Docks, like sorrels, contain oxalic acid and so should not be eaten in large quantities.**

# Elder
## (*Sambucus nigra*)

There is much folklore associated with the elder (trees were grown by the house to keep the Devil away, for example). It also has a long history of medicinal use. It is a common host of the jelly-ear fungus (*Auricularia auricula-judae*), an edible fungus which can look disturbingly ear-like and has a jelly-like feel to it. Elderberries have a high antioxidant content and are a good source of vitamin C. Elder orchards were once widely grown in the Kent region and the berries used in wines.

## Appearance and habitat

Elder (sometimes known as European black elder) is a shrub or small tree that is native to Europe, North Africa and south-west Asia. It has deep-green leaves with 3-9 leaflets and flat-topped heads of cream flowers with a strong musky scent. It usually flowers around June and the berries ripen in August or September. The English summer is traditionally said to begin when the elder blooms and end when the berries ripen. The shiny purple-black fruits are smaller than blackcurrants but just as popular with birds. Various ornamental forms have been selected from the wild and are in cultivation, including 'Aurea', which has golden leaves, and 'Thundercloud', with rich reddish-black foliage and deep-pink flowers.

Elder is a hardy and adaptable plant that tolerates a variety of soil types and will grow in shady locations. This adaptability and the freedom with which wild birds spread the seeds enables it to spread widely and it is a common weed species in gardens, scrub and wasteland.

## Uses

The flowers of the elder are regularly made into cordials, both at home and commercially. The cordial is used with vodka and champagne to make a cocktail known as the twinkle. Elderflower champagne, a clear sparkling drink, is also popular; there are both lightly alcoholic and non-alcoholic versions. The flowers can also be used to flavour desserts such as sorbets and syllabubs.

The berries can be used in cordials or to make a rich and full-bodied hedgerow wine, best drunk when mature. They are ideal for country jams and preserves, pies, cakes and crumbles, either on their own or with apples and other berries such as blackberries. There is a high proportion of pip to fruit, so jelly recipes in which the pulp is strained through muslin may be preferred to jams. Remove the berries from the stalks before using. This is most easily done by cutting the whole heads of berries then combing off the individual berries with a fork.

The jelly-ear fungus can be simmered in butter and served perhaps with a beef and elderberry casserole.

## Related plants

Elder was formerly considered to be a member of the honeysuckle family (Caprifoliaceae), but has now been placed with viburnums in the Adoxaceae family.

CAUTION: The flowers and berries are edible when cooked but are sometimes said to be poisonous raw. My youngest son was unaffected by eating a handful of raw berries straight off the tree when he was a toddler, but there are reports of as few as two berries causing gastrointestinal upsets. Do not eat the roots, stalks or leaves of the elder as they contain poisonous glycosides. Elder is rarely eaten by grazing animals and the leaves have been used woven into the headbands of horses to keep away flies.

There are around a dozen different species of *Sambucus* but it is not advisable to try eating those other than *S. nigra*, as they may contain toxic levels of cyanide-producing glycosides. Certainly drinking tea made from the dwarf elder, *S. ebulus* (a herbaceous species to 1.5m (5') tall which dies back in winter) has been known to cause vomiting and diarrhoea.[8]

The leaves of any elder species, including *S. nigra*, should not be eaten.

# Elderflower champagne

Approximate preparation time: 1 hour, plus time to infuse and mature

Bucket or trugful of elderflower heads
2 lemons, chopped
3 litres (100fl oz / 5¼ pints) water
680g (1lb 8oz) sugar
2 tbsp white wine vinegar

1  Rinse flowers to remove any wildlife and put into clean bucket with lemons and water. Allow to steep for 24 hours.

2  Strain through muslin and add the sugar and vinegar to the resulting liquid.

3  Stir until the sugar is completely dissolved, then decant into sterile screw-top bottles, leaving the lids slightly loose for the first 2 weeks. Allow to mature for 2-3 months before drinking.

# Elderflower rice pudding

Serves 4
Approximate preparation time: 1 hour

570ml (20fl oz / 1 pint) milk
6 elderflower heads
50g (1¾oz) sugar
50g (1¾oz) short-grain pudding rice
100ml (3½fl oz) double cream
2 tbsp demerara sugar

1  Pour the milk into a heavy-based saucepan, then add the flowerheads. Bring the mixture to the boil, turn off the heat, then allow to infuse for around half an hour.

2  Strain through a sieve and return the milk to the pan. Add the sugar and boil until the sugar has dissolved.

3  Stir in the rice and cook over a very low heat for 8-10 minutes, stirring regularly, until the rice is tender. Stir in the double cream. Sprinkle over the demerara sugar and caramelise the sugar under a hot grill.

# Elderberry fritters

Serves 4
Approximate preparation time: 30 minutes

2 tbsp plain flour
285ml (10fl oz / ½ pint) milk
4 eggs
1 tbsp sugar
3 tbsp boiled rice
3 tbsp elderberries
Vegetable oil

1  Mix flour with a little of the milk to form a paste then whisk in the rest of the milk with the eggs and sugar.

2  Stir in the rice and elderberries.

3  Heat the oil in a pan and fry spoonfuls of the mixture until golden brown. Serve hot, with a wedge of lemon and dusted with sifted icing sugar.

# Spiced Yorkshire puddings with elderberry compote

Serves about 4
Approximate preparation time: 40 minutes

*For the compote:*
200g (7oz) elderberries, destalked
200g (7oz) sugar

*For the puddings:*
2 eggs
100g (3½oz) plain flour
150ml (5½fl oz) milk
1 tsp cinnamon

1  To make the compote, rinse the elderberries and put in a pan with the sugar. Do not add any extra water.

2  Gently heat until the sugar has dissolved in the juices that will run from the berries, then boil for 5 minutes. Allow to cool.

3  To make the puddings, beat the ingredients together to a smooth batter.

4  Using two four-hole Yorkshire pudding tins, pour a little oil in each and put in a hot oven (220°C / 425°F / Gas Mark 7) to get very hot.

5  Carefully take the tins out and divide the batter between them. Cook for about 20 minutes until well risen and golden.

6  Serve with a spoonful of compote in each pudding and accompany with cream or a good vanilla ice cream.

# Fat hen
## (*Chenopodium album*)

One of the most abundant and wide-spread annual weeds, fat hen has been cultivated as a food crop since ancient times. The seeds have been recovered from Neolithic sites throughout northern Europe. The gruel that formed the last meal of Tollund Man in Denmark (400 BC) included seeds of fat hen along with a number of other wild and cultivated plants. Fat hen was known as melde in Anglo-Saxon times, when it was still considered an important food crop. It was certainly important enough to give its name to the village of Milden in Suffolk, which was known as Meldinges in the twelfth century. The villagers have commemorated the weed in a sculpture for their village sign.

Fat hen is a richer source of protein and iron than spinach and is particularly high in magnesium.[9] It is very high in vitamin C, with reports giving values of 84-171mg per 100g of leaves.

## Appearance and habitat

Fat hen grows best on fertile clay and loam soils and is commonly found among arable crops, on waste ground and roadsides, and, of course, in gardens. The common name dung weed refers to its habit of growing on manure heaps. It prefers to grow in sunny places. It is a variable species of erect habit usually growing between 30 and 60cm (1' and 2') high, although if conditions are suitable it can reach as much as 2m (6'6") tall.

The seed leaves and first true leaves have a mealy silvery appearance. Older leaves are deep green with pale undersides and are very roughly diamond-shaped with toothed margins. The stems are often reddish. It flowers from July to October with dense clusters of minute green flowers, and a single healthy plant can produce 75,000 seeds.

**CAUTION:** Care must be taken when eating fat hen, as it contains high levels of oxalates, which can cause problems with calcium metabolism. Levels are said to be lower in young plants and increase until flowering time. The oxalates have been responsible for incidents of poisoning in grazing animals, though this is only likely to occur if large quantities are consumed. Affected animals become listless, with shallow breathing and a weak heartbeat.

There have been occasional cases of photosensitisation in humans, in which exposure of the skin to sunlight after eating the plant has caused swelling and blistering of the skin. Plants have a deep taproot and can potentially accumulate harmful levels of nitrates from the soil.

## Uses

The leaves can be eaten fresh in salads or cooked as a side vegetable. Fat hen is a useful vegetable for soups and risottos or can be used in quiches or scattered over pizzas. In northern India fat hen is known as *bathua* and it is widely eaten steamed as a winter vegetable. It is mixed with other greens and lentils to make dahls and is used as a stuffing for pakoras.

The seeds are known to have been ground for flour and the leaves were widely used as a green vegetable before the introduction of spinach. Spinach and fat hen are both members of the Chenopodiaceae family. Spinach, which was introduced to Spain by the Arabs in AD 1100, has milder tasting, more tender leaves than its wild cousin but it is less drought-tolerant.

Fat hen can also be used as a dye plant giving a 'blonde' dye when using alum and cream of tartar as mordants.

## Related species

*Chenopodium giganteum* is a native of India and can grow as much as 2.5m (8') tall so the common name of tree spinach is not entirely unexpected. It is a very attractive plant as the new growth is flushed a rich magenta-purple colour. It is often grown as a garden

Tree spinach is quite ornamental.

plant and once allowed to seed will usually reappear each year. *C. capi-tatum*, known as the strawberry blite, is a native of North America but has been widely cultivated and so can sometimes turn up as a weed in gardens. Its rich-red flowers grow in clusters somewhat resembling straw-berries. Flowers and leaves of both species can be eaten, but as with fat hen they should be used in moderation as they are also high in oxalates.

## Bathua raita

Serves about 4
Approximate preparation time: 15 minutes

170ml (6fl oz) fat hen leaves
170ml (6fl oz) natural yogurt
1 tsp cumin powder
Pinch of chilli powder

1  Boil the fat hen leaves for 5 minutes.

2  Drain and squeeze the water out of them.

3  Stir the yogurt, leaves and spices together into a smooth paste. Serve as a dip with chapattis or nachos.

## Fat hen frittata

Serves 4
Approximate preparation time: 30 minutes

400g (14oz) fat hen
1 clove garlic, crushed
1 tsp olive oil
Pinch of nutmeg
6 eggs
200ml (7fl oz) milk
1 tbsp plain flour
1 tbsp Parmesan cheese, grated
Ground black pepper
30g (1oz) butter

1  Wash the fat hen thoroughly, then heat it in a pan with no added water until it wilts.

2  Drain well and fry it with the garlic, olive oil and the nutmeg.

3  Beat the eggs in a bowl, then stir in the milk, flour and cheese. Add the fat hen and black pepper.

4  Heat the butter in a pan and add the egg mixture, shaking the pan briskly to settle the ingredients evenly.

5  Cook the frittata slowly over a gentle heat until the top begins to set, then finish under a grill to brown. Divide into slices and serve hot or cold with crusty bread and a salad.

# Garden orache
## (*Atriplex hortensis*)

Garden orache, also known as mountain spinach or French spinach, has been used as food since Mesolithic times. It is said to have been introduced to Britain in 1548. The leaves have a higher protein content than many other green vegetables, and also contain vitamin C, and the seeds have protein levels similar to those of legume vegetables such as peas. However, oraches contain oxalic acid, and so should be eaten only in moderation.

## Appearance and habitat

A fast-growing hardy annual with triangular leaves with a grey mealy coating, garden orache is thought to be native to Asia. It can grow as much as 1.8m (6') tall in just a few months. The leaves are tender and tasty so plants were introduced initially for edible purposes.[10] Oraches are very tolerant of drought and of salty environments – the leaves can accumulate salts and so may have a savoury taste.

There are forms with rose-red or purple-flushed foliage that are often grown ornamentally, but are just as edible as the plain green form. Orache spreads readily by seed.

## Uses

The soft-textured leaves have a mild spinach-like taste. They are delicious raw in salads. Young shoots and leaves can also be cooked. Boil for only a short time until they have just wilted in order to retain the water-soluble vitamins. The red-leaved forms retain their colour when cooked. The texture can be somewhat mucilaginous and so they can be added to thicken soups and stews. The fat seeds can be scattered over salads.

## Related species

Other *Atriplex* species can be used in the same way, including *A. patula*, *A. nummularia* and *A. cinerea*.

# Goat's beard
## (*Tragopogon pratensis*)

An alternative name for goat's beard is 'Jack-go-to-bed-at-noon' because of the behaviour of its flowers, which come out at daybreak and close by midday. As the seeds start to form, the silvery plumes protrude and are meant to look like a goat's beard. The sweet taste is due to a high concentration of inulin, which is a storage carbohydrate that acts as a source of soluble dietary fibre in the body. It is thought to be of benefit in facilitating calcium uptake.[11]

## Appearance and habitat

Goat's beard is a biennial or short-lived perennial plant with flowers similar to those of dandelions but with long, pointed green bracts. It can be distinguished from other dandelion-like plants by the narrow grassy leaves. If the stems are damaged they ooze a milky sap. It grows on road verges, fields and wasteland across Europe and has naturalised in North America. The flowers are held on tall stems to around 70cm (2'4") high. The most conspicuous feature of the plant is the seedhead, which looks like a particularly beefy dandelion seedhead, up to 7cm (3") across.

## Uses

Mrs Beeton reported that the roots of goat's beard, when dug before the stems start to shoot, can be boiled like asparagus and have the same flavour. Dig the roots in the autumn or any time over the winter or early spring so long as the ground is not frozen. The roots should be gently scraped to remove the outer peel. Cut them into finger-length pieces and drop them into water to which a little lemon juice has been added to prevent discolouration. Boil in water until tender, drain and serve in a white sauce or with melted butter. Alternatively, they can be dipped in beaten egg then in breadcrumbs, and fried in butter for an interesting side dish.

The shoots and young flower buds are also edible. Break off the buds with a section of the stem. Harvesting them is quite a sticky job as the white sap tends to get all over your fingers, but it is worthwhile as they are delicious with a mild asparagus flavour and a hint of sweetness.

## Related plants

*Tragopogon porrifolius* is a purple-flowered species from the Mediterranean region, which also only flowers in the morning. It is taller than goat's beard, growing up to 120cm (4'). It has been cultivated since ancient times as a winter root vegetable known as salsify or the oyster plant, and has naturalised widely in Europe and the USA. The roots are delicious if simply boiled and served as a side vegetable or used in gratins. The young shoots of overwintered plants, known as chards, are also edible, as are the flower buds. The latter should be picked with a

short length of stem, just before they open. They are cooked and eaten as asparagus.

The name 'goat's beard' is also used for *Aruncus dioicus*, a plant in the rose family.

CAUTION: Large quantities of inulin-containing foods can cause a bloating sensation if your body is not used to them, so they are best introduced to the diet gradually.

Do not confuse goat's beard with goat's rue (*Galega officinalis*), which is a member of the pea family. This ornamental plant with mauve or white flowers has caused cases of poisoning in grazing animals.

# Good King Henry
## (*Chenopodium bonus-henricus*)

Good King Henry is native to most of Europe but has been grown as a green vegetable since early times and self-seeds freely, so many apparently wild plants may be relics of cultivation. The common name was originally Good Henry, which served to distinguish it from the very poisonous Bad Henry, which is now usually called dog's mercury (see page 46). The alternative name of Lincolnshire spinach arose as it was commonly grown as a vegetable in the gardens of Lincolnshire in the nineteenth century. It can be blanched by inverting a bucket over it to give long pale shoots. Both leaves and flowering shoots contain high levels of anti-oxidants.

## Appearance and habitat

Good King Henry is a member of the group of plants known as goosefoots. It is found particularly on rich fertile soils such as manure heaps, farmyards and animal pasture and is also common on salt marshes and near the seashore. It is a perennial species with triangular, spear-shaped leaves that are sometimes tinged red. Mature plants can reach about 60cm (2') high. They have spikes of greenish flowers from May to July, which produce many thousands of extremely small seeds.

Leave a couple of plants to grow in a shady spot in the garden where few other vegetables succeed. They are drought-tolerant and rarely bothered by pests or diseases and so are easy to grow.

## Uses

The leaves can be picked continually, making this a good cut-and-come-again vegetable. They wilt readily once cut and so are unlikely to ever appear on the supermarket shelves. Cook the leaves as you would spinach. Some are fairly mild tasting, but depending on season and growing conditions they can be rather bitter. If so, soak in salted water for an hour or so then rinse before cooking. They are excellent with oily fish such as mackerel, used as a filling for pancakes or in quiches and omelettes.

The young shoots can be harvested when they are 15-20cm (6-8") tall. Simmer in water for 5 minutes and serve with melted butter. They are considered to be a poor man's (or frugal forager's) asparagus. The unopened flower buds can be served as a broccoli substitute.

## Related species

The genus *Chenopodium* contains some 150 species of plants, commonly known as goosefoots from the shape of their leaves. Many species have been used as foods since prehistoric times. Goosefoot fruits were found preserved in a basket in Russell Cave, Alabama, suggesting deliberate storage of the seeds for spring sowing, and are thought to date to before 1000 BC. The seeds found had thinner seed coats than wild plants, indicating domestication of the plant.

*Chenopodium quinoa* is a staple food in the Andes region in South America. It was known by the Incas as *chisaya mama*, 'mother of all grains'. It is currently attracting scientific interest as the grain-like seeds are gluten-free and so suitable for use by people with coeliac disease. Most quinoa grain sold has been processed by soaking and rinsing to reduce the levels of saponins that it contains. A high-quality oil obtained from the seeds has similar properties to corn oil.

**CAUTION: As with other goosefoots, Good King Henry has a relatively high oxalate content. Safe consumption levels have not been assessed, although studies are ongoing due to the possibility of high oxalate levels causing kidney stones.**

# Goosegrass
## (*Galium aparine*)

plant exhibits by virtue of the covering of tiny hooks which attach themselves like Velcro® to other plants or passing animals.

The scientific name *Galium* is derived from *gala*, the Greek word for 'milk' (which also gives the name *Galanthus* to the snowdrop). The Greek physician Dioscorides reported that shepherds used the rough stems of galiums to strain impurities from milk, although another possible origin for the name is that they contain enzymes which can be used as vegetable rennets to curdle milk. According to the English herbalist John Gerard, the people of Nantwich thought that the best cheeses were made with goosegrass rennet. The seventeenth-century herbalist Nicholas Culpeper recommended the juice of goosegrass in a glass of wine to help those bitten by adders, although nowadays your nearest emergency hospital may have different ideas.

Goosegrass has a long association with humans, as indicated by the legion of common names for it, including beggar's lice, catchweed bedstraw, cleavers, everlasting friendship, gosling weed, grip grass, herriff, kisses, stick-a-back and sticky Willy. Many of these names refer to the adhesive nature that the

Eight different flavonoid compounds have been identified from goosegrass plants. These are thought to have antioxidant properties.

## Appearance and habitat

Goosegrass is a common and distinctive hedgerow plant found through most of the northern hemisphere. It is an annual, germinating early in the year and growing rapidly into dense tangles which can smother surrounding vegetation and grow up into shrubs and trees to a height of 1.5m (5') or more. The leaves are arranged in whorls around square stems. The tiny, starry white flowers are quite insignificant, and give way to numerous hard, spherical fruits which ripen from green to a dull brown.

Individual plants growing in rich soil can produce more than 3,000 fruits. The plant has an extensive root system and cutting it back to ground level stimulates a lot of regrowth from the root. This is useful if you want to treat it as a cut-and-come-again vegetable, but irritating if you are trying to get rid of it.

## Uses

Goosegrass is theoretically edible raw, with a mild grass-like flavour, but even when very young the tiny hooks on the leaves can catch at the back of your throat and make you gag. However, after just a couple of seconds' boiling or steaming the hooks disintegrate and the plant can be used as a prolific source of spring greens. It is best to pick the young growth before the plant starts to flower otherwise it begins to get a bit stringy. Cook and use as you would spinach.

A herbal tea can be prepared by steeping a couple of teaspoons of the chopped plant in a cup of hot water. For those who like to drink vegetable juices, juicing generous handfuls of goosegrass with tomatoes and celery yields a refreshing drink. Unfortunately, juicing the leaves reduces the vitamin C content due to oxidation of the ascorbic acid on exposure to air when the plant tissues are damaged. It is best therefore to drink the juice as soon as it is made.

The roots of goosegrass produce a red dye known as galiosin. This is similar to the dye derived from madder, which was used to produce the scarlet tunics of British soldiers. As the common name suggests it is also a useful fodder crop for geese and chickens.

## Related plants

In the same genus as goosegrass are sweet woodruff (*Galium odoratum*) and lady's bedstraw (*G. verum*). The dried foliage of sweet woodruff has an attractive fragrance and it was much used as a strewing herb in the Middle Ages. Stuffed into herb pillows, it is said to be effective against insomnia. Lady's bedstraw has frothy yellow flowers which are scented of honey. It was widely used to stuff mattresses as it was said to repel fleas. The wider madder family (Rubiaceae) includes the Arabian coffee plant; indeed, the dried fruit of goosegrass can be roasted and ground to be used as a caffeine-free coffee substitute.

# Ground elder
## (*Aegopodium podagraria*)

It is thought that ground elder was probably introduced to Britain as a pot-herb but it has spread extensively and is now a pervasive, troublesome garden weed. It is also known as goutweed as it was considered to be a cure for gout. It contains useful amounts of minerals such as iron and manganese, and is a source of vitamin C.

## Appearance and habitat

Native to most of the temperate regions of Europe and Asia, ground elder is a herbaceous perennial that spreads by long, white, creeping rhizomes. It is a woodland plant growing to around 50cm (1'8") high and has deep-green leaves divided into threes, with toothed edges. It is not closely related to the shrubby elder (*Sambucus nigra*) but was called ground elder due to the similarity of the leaves. The flat heads of lacy white flowers bloom from May to July.

The rhizomes can spread by a metre or more a year, and the plant can also establish itself elsewhere by seed. It forms a dense ground cover which will aggressively out-compete most other perennial plants. There is a variegated form, *Aegopodium podagraria* 'Variegatum', sold by several nurserymen who claim that due to its relative lack of chlorophyll it will bring light to shady corners without running riot. Do not be fooled: it may indeed take longer to get established but it still has world domination on its mind.

## Control

Organic control is very difficult because the white rhizomes are very brittle and it is essential to remove every scrap or they will regrow. Do not compost the rhizomes as you may end up distributing them further around the garden. Put them in a black plastic bag, add some water then leave them to thoroughly rot down before adding to the compost heap. A very deep mulch may smother growth, but it needs to be left in place for several seasons. If you are very persistent then repeatedly removing all leaves will weaken and eventually kill the plant, but most gardeners resort to a glyphosate-based weedkiller or just learn to live with a ground elder ground cover.

Ground elder boiled as a green vegetable.

## Uses

Ground elder has a long history of use as a medicinal herb, not only for the treatment of gout but also as a poultice for burns and stings.

Fresh young leaves picked when they are just opening and still shiny can be eaten raw in salads. They have a rich aromatic flavour that tends to linger on your tongue. Mature leaves are better eaten cooked and can be boiled like spinach or incorporated into soups and stews. The flavour works well in egg dishes such as omelettes or the classic Dr Seuss recipe, green eggs and ham.

## Green eggs and ham

Serves 4 as a starter or light supper snack
Approximate preparation time: 30 minutes

200g (7oz) ground elder
Butter
4 large eggs
50g (1¾oz) thick ham, diced
Ground black pepper
150ml (5½fl oz) cream
30g (1oz) Parmesan cheese, grated

1  Blanch the ground elder in lightly salted water for 2 or 3 minutes, drain and rinse.

2  Butter four ramekins or French cocotte dishes, stand them on a baking tray and divide the ground elder between them.

3  Break an egg into each dish then scatter over the ham.

4  Beat some black pepper into the cream then pour over the eggs.

5  Sprinkle with cheese and bake in a medium oven (180°C / 350°F / Gas Mark 4) for 15-20 minutes until the cream is bubbling and the eggs set. Serve with crusty bread.

# Hairy bittercress
## (*Cardamine hirsuta*)

In the tenth-century Lacnunga manuscript, lamb's cress was one of nine herbs used as a charm to counteract poisons. The slim, elongated seedpods split with an explosive force at the slightest touch, propelling the seeds over a wide area. This volatile nature has earned the plant common names such as don't sneeze, flickweed, jumping Jesus, popping cress and touch-me-not. Cardamine leaves are about 14 per cent protein, which is higher than many other green vegetables. The vitamin C content is comparable to that of cabbage.

## Appearance and habitat

A common annual weed in gardens and on waste ground throughout Europe and Asia, hairy bittercress or lamb's cress is a low-growing plant with rosettes of divided leaves and clusters of small white flowers. It has been introduced to America and is now widespread there. Flowers appear through most of the year and the plant is very quick to set seed, often in just 6 weeks from germinating. The seeds become sticky when damp and will stick to shoes and garden tools and so are easily spread around the garden. Plants often have a purplish tint to them, which can make them quite tricky to spot against the soil in flowerbeds.

## Uses

Although bittercress is often considered the nurseryman's despair due to the prolific way it spreads its seeds around, it is valuable as a source of salad leaves early in the year, being quite hardy and resistant to frost. The whole plant can be eaten, though the flowering stalks can be rather fibrous. Although the name bittercress sounds off-putting, it is not really bitter but has a peppery taste, milder than that of rocket. It is used in place of cress to give a tangy taste to salads and egg sandwiches, and is good in recipes with cream cheeses. Lightly steaming or cooking tends to reduce the peppery character of the leaves.

Bittercress is sometimes used as a green manure but because of the rapid rate at which it can set seed, great care must be taken to make sure that it is dug into the soil before it flowers.

## Related species

Wavy bittercress (*Cardamine flexuosa*) is a similar but taller species, more common in moister locations. It occasionally survives as a perennial plant. New Zealand bittercress (*C. corymbosa*) has been recently introduced to the northern hemisphere through the nursery trade. It makes a nuisance of itself in potted plants and by spreading rapidly in polytunnels. It is a similar-looking species but is a brighter shade of green and tends to be more difficult to weed out as it hugs the ground particularly tightly.

The more ornamental lady's smock or cuckoo flower (*C. pratensis*) can also be eaten and has a slightly stronger flavour.

### Bittercress and cream cheese quiche

Serves 4-6 (or 24 tartlets for party food)
Approximate preparation time: 45 minutes

200g (7oz) puff pastry
2 eggs
200g (7oz) soft cream cheese
1 tbsp paprika
Generous handful of hairy bittercress

**1**  Roll out the pastry and use to line a 20cm (8") flan ring or two 12-cup tart tins.

**2**  Beat the eggs with the cream cheese and paprika.

**3**  Put the bittercress in the bottom of the pastry case and pour over the egg and cheese mixture. Bake in a medium oven (180°C / 350°F / Gas Mark 4) for around 20-30 minutes until golden.

# Himalayan balsam
## (*Impatiens glandulifera*)

Widely naturalised in Europe and North America, the species was introduced to British gardens from the Himalaya in 1839 and has proved to be a very invasive species. It now dominates large areas of riverbanks throughout the country. As with other balsam species, the seeds are ejected explosively from the ripe seed capsules at the slightest touch. It is this way of violently discharging the ripe seeds from the pod that gave the plant the botanical name *Impatiens*, from the Latin for 'impatient'. Seeds can be shot as far as 7m (23') away. Each plant can produce as many as 800 seeds. The seeds themselves are light and corky so they float on water until they lodge on muddy banks downstream. The seeds have quite a high oil content.

## Appearance and habitat

Himalayan balsam is a relative of the popular bedding plant busy Lizzie. It is a dramatic plant growing to around 2m (6'6") tall with red-tinged stems and leaves and masses of pink, lavender or rose-purple flowers. The hooded shape of the flowers has earned the plant the alternative common name of policeman's helmet. It blooms from July to October with a heavy scent and is popular with bumblebees.

## Control

While it is undoubtedly an attractive plant, its aggressive spread and ability to crowd out native species makes it unpopular with conservationists, and many Wildlife Trusts hold regular 'balsam bashing' events to try to keep it under control. Plants are best hand pulled, as the use of weedkillers alongside waterways is inadvisable.

## Uses

The seedpods are edible raw, if you can catch them before they explode. They have a sweet, nutty flavour and make an interesting snack food if you are out walking. Once ripe the seeds can be collected (but beware they do not catch you in the eyes) and used in savoury snacks.

The flowers do not have much taste but are extremely attractive scattered over salads. They can be used to make a very attractive pink jam or in the Indian preserve known as *gulqand*, which literally means 'sweet flowers'. Leaves and young shoots can be boiled then added to stir-fries or curries.

## Related species

Orange balsam, *Impatiens capensis*, is a North American species, first found wild in Britain in 1822. It has naturalised along canals and riverbanks. In its native America, where it is known as jewelweed, the mucilaginous fluid that oozes from broken stems is used to soothe the irritation of stinging nettles. Small balsam, *I. parviflora*, is a native of Siberia and Turkestan but has naturalised over much of Europe, often growing in woodland and shady riverbanks. It has small yellow flowers that are usually pollinated by hover-flies. Use the flowers and seeds of these species in the same way as those of Himalayan balsam.

**CAUTION: All balsams contain calcium oxalate crystals, so they should not be eaten regularly or in large quantities.[12]**

## Balsam straws

Approximate preparation time: 30 minutes

100g (3½oz) butter or margarine
200g (7oz) plain flour
50g (1¾oz) Parmesan cheese, grated
1 tsp paprika
1 tbsp Himalayan balsam seeds

1  Rub the fat into the flour until the mixture resembles breadcrumbs.

2  Stir in the other ingredients then add sufficient water to make a firm dough. Cover and refrigerate for 15 minutes.

3  Roll out to around 1cm (about ½") thick and cut into finger-sized straws. Bake in a hot oven (220°C / 425°F / Gas Mark 7) until golden brown.

# Hop
## (*Humulus lupulus*)

The hop is a wild plant of hedgerows and the edges of woodland, particularly on loamy soils throughout temperate Europe and Asia. However, it has been cultivated for more than 1,000 years and many apparently wild plants may be relics of cultivation, as hop growing was once far more extensive than it is today. Seedlings often turn up in the garden but are fairly easily removed if unwanted. The plants spread by rhizomatous shoots from the main rootstock. Digging around a mature plant in early spring reveals lots of these narrow white or pinkish shoots, which were known as poor man's asparagus because they can be eaten in the same way. The female flowers of the hop plant contain high levels of essential oils and antioxidant vitamins, including C and E.

## Appearance and habitat

A perennial climbing plant usually reaching 3-6m (10-20') tall, the hop dies back to ground level each winter. The large, deep-green leaves have deep lobes, similar to those of grape vines. A yellow-leaved form, *Humulus lupulus* 'Aureus', is often grown as an ornamental, and a large number of different brewers' cultivars have been selected for growing in different regions of the world.

In the northern hemisphere hops flower in July and August. There are separate male and female plants. The male plants have small starry flowers, while those of females carry the familiar cone-like bracts. In hop-growing areas the desired female cultivars are propagated vegetatively and any male plants found are usually removed in order to prevent seed formation and maintain a genetically consistent crop. It is the bracts that secrete the mixture of aromatic oils and resins known as lupulin that gives the distinctive scent to beer.

## Uses

Lupulin is widely reported to have a sedative effect. The use of hops as an aid to sleep was popularised when a pillow filled with hops was used to cure George III of his insomnia. Hop pillows are still in use today, often in combination with lavender. Alternatively, a muslin bag full of hops can be hung under the hot tap when filling a bath, to aid relaxation.

Hops can, of course, be used in home brewing, but the new shoots are also edible as a vegetable. Dig the rhizomes in late winter or early spring, or cut the young emerging shoots when they are around 15-20cm (6-8") long. Remove any large leaves then soak in salt water for an hour or so to reduce bitterness. Drain and rinse then boil for just a few minutes until tender. Serve as you would asparagus, with melted butter, or use in soups, quiches and omelettes. It is worth harvesting them if only for the fun of saying "chops and buttered hop tops" when the children ask what is for supper. In France, where they are known as *jets de houblon*, hop shoots are considered a delicacy, and are often served with a cream sauce.

To use the bracts, harvest them in late August or September. For commercial purposes they would be immediately dried by forced hot air, but for home use hang boughs of bracts in a warm, dark, airy space such as a spare bedroom or potting shed. Alternatively, spread the bracts out over a sheet of metal gauze. Allow to dry for up to a week then test; if the stems are brittle and break rather than bend, they are ready to use or store.

## Related plants

The hop family (Cannabaceae) includes the well-known plant hemp, from which the illegal drug cannabis is obtained. It was much cultivated in medieval times as a medicinal herb and a source of hemp fibre. The seeds of hemp can be used to produce an oil that, like fish oils, contains a high proportion of essential fatty acids including omega-6 and omega-3 fatty acids, which are thought to be protective against heart disease. Hempseed oil has a relatively low smoke point and is not suitable for frying, but used in salad dressings could be a useful part of the diet, particularly for those who do not consume oily fish. The strains grown for fibre and oil today do not develop a significant amount of tetrahydrocannabinol, the narcotic ingredient, but in the UK and most other countries they still may only be cultivated under licence.

# Horseradish
## (*Armoracia rusticana*)

Thought to have originated in southern Russia and eastern Ukraine, horseradish was widely cultivated for culinary and medicinal purposes by the Middle Ages. Having escaped from cultivation, the plant can now be commonly found throughout Europe and North America. It is very popular in Eastern Europe, where it is eaten served at traditional Easter meals. Fresh horseradish is very high in vitamin C; however, levels will reduce upon exposure to air when the root is grated.

## Appearance and habitat

Once identified, horseradish is easy to spot on roadsides, wasteland and railway embankments, forming thick clumps of large robust leaves that grow to 60cm (2') or more long. They are a rich, deep glossy green with wavy edges, and could be mistaken for those of a robust dock plant. It sends up airy stems of snow-white flowers in early summer, but seed is seldom set in Britain. There is an ornamental cultivar 'Variegata', which has dramatic leaves splashed with cream.

## Uses

Very young fresh leaves can be harvested in springtime and used as a zesty green vegetable, but as they mature they quickly get very bitter.

The long tapering root can be harvested from October through to June, when it starts to flower. It is at its most potent in October and November. On sandy soils you may be able to pull up the plant, but generally harvesting the deep taproot requires some serious spadework. The pungent roots must then be peeled and grated, which is a job best done outdoors and while wearing gloves.

There are many recipes for horseradish sauce, but the simplest method is to mix the grated horseradish with an equal volume of sour cream to which a little mustard and sugar is added.

Horeseradish sauce, with its hot, biting, pungent taste, is a classic accompaniment to roast beef and boiled tongue, but horseradish can also be mixed with vinegar and served with fish or added to mustards or mayonnaise.

**CAUTION: The root and leaves contain a chemical called sinigrin, which is hydrolysed to allyl isothiocyanate, a potent irritant of eyes and skin. Do not allow animals to graze where horseradish is growing as there have been occasional deaths of horses and cattle. If harvesting over winter when leaves are not present, it is very important that you are sure of the plant; a death occurred in Germany one December, when someone dug up the extremely toxic aconite root (*Aconitum napellus*) instead of horseradish.[13] It is, however, a strange mistake to make, as aconites do not give off the distinctive, extremely pungent aroma of horseradish.**

## Horseradish rarebit

Serves 1
Approximate preparation time: 15 minutes

2 thick slices bread
100g (3½oz) cheddar cheese, grated
1 spring onion, chopped
1 tsp horseradish, grated
3 tbsp beer

1  Toast the bread.

2  Mix all the other ingredients together with a fork. Spread the mixture over the toasted bread, ensuring you cover right up to the edges so that they do not burn.

3  Place under a medium grill and cook until the cheese is starting to bubble and brown. Serve with a salad garnish.

# Hottentot fig
## (*Carpobrotus edulis*)

A native of South Africa, the hottentot fig is a succulent plant that has escaped from cultivation and become naturalised in many other parts of the world. In some places it was deliberately planted to stabilise sand dunes, but has since run wild. Even small fragments of the plant can grow to new individuals, and it spreads very rapidly although hard frosts will damage its growth. The spread on cliffs is thought to be in part due to seabirds using the pieces as nesting material.

The term 'hottentot' was used by European immigrants to southern Africa to describe the Khoikhoi people. It is now considered a derogatory term. In South Africa, hottentot figs are usually referred to simply as sour figs. The figs contain high levels of tannins, which can have antioxidant and antibacterial properties, but they may reduce the absorption of nutrients such as calcium from the gut.

## Appearance and habitat

In the British Isles, hottentot figs are widespread on coastal cliffs and dunes in the south-west and on the Channel Islands. It is invasive in Australia, California and many parts of the Mediterranean coast.

The low, sprawling stems have paired, narrow succulent leaves and daisy-like flowers to 9cm (3½") across. They have yellow, yellowish-pink or magenta petals and a centre of yellow stamens. Yellow and magenta flowers can occur on the same plant. In the northern hemisphere it generally flowers from May to July. Once the flower fades, the receptacle enlarges to become a fleshy fruit that is somewhat fig-like. Slicing it open reveals a sticky interior with many small seeds.

## Uses

The figs can be eaten straight off the plant – just cut or bite the end off and suck out the pulpy flesh. They have an interesting tart-salty taste. In South Africa they are made into a jam. To try this, collect the figs in midsummer before they are too dry and shrivelled. They make an unusual preserve to spoon over waffles or to stir into porridge.

The leaves are also edible, but have an astringent taste due to the high tannin content. Pricking the leaves with a pin or slicing into triangles, then leaving them to soak overnight in salted water before rinsing, will reduce the astringency but is somewhat laborious. If you have time on your hands in the summer and want to try it, you can pickle prepared leaves by boiling them in vinegar with black peppercorns for a minute or two, then bottling in glass jars.

## Related species

*Carpobrotus quadrifidus*, from the Strandveld on the western coast of South Africa, has larger flowers, and fruit which can be much sweeter.

### Sour fig jam

Approximate preparation time: 1 hour, plus soaking time

500g (1lb 2oz) hottentot figs
500ml (18fl oz) water
500g (1lb 2oz) sugar
1 tbsp lemon juice

**1** Cut stalks and any loose leaves from the figs and soak overnight in lightly salted water.

**2** Rinse well and drain. Those of an industrious nature may wish to remove the skins at this stage for the best results, but it is a fiddly job.

**3** Boil all the ingredients together over a medium heat until the figs are tender and the liquid syrupy. Bottle into sterile jars, and seal.

# Ivy-leaved toadflax
## (*Cymbalaria muralis*)

A native of southern Europe, ivy-leaved toadflax was introduced to Britain in the seventeenth century. The nutrient content of the leaves varies depending on growing conditions: plants in urban areas tend to have lower concentrations of calcium than plants in rural situations, while zinc concentrations are higher in urban sites. Plants growing beside roads should be avoided as they may show high concentrations of heavy metals due to traffic pollution.

## Appearance and habitat

This is a very common weed on old walls in town and countryside. It is a creeping perennial with long, trailing stems that are often purplish in colour and small pale-violet spurred flowers. Once pollinated, the flowerheads bend away from the light so that the seeds are deposited into cracks in the wall. Plants look deceptively delicate but this is a robust species that in rockeries can soon smother other plants.

## Uses

The leaves and lengths of trailing stems can be added to mixed salads. The leaves are fleshy with a cress-like flavour and they can be used as a substitute for cress in sandwiches and quiches or as a garnish for buffet foods or soups.

## Related plants

Toadflaxes are members of the Plantaginaceae (formerly Scrophulariaceae) family, which includes the foxglove, well known for its poisonous qualities.

**CAUTION: Other family members, including common toadflax (*Linaria vulgaris*), contain poisonous glycosides, which could cause illness if eaten in large quantities.**

# Jack-by-the-hedge
## (*Alliaria petiolata*)

Jack-by-the-hedge, as the name suggests, is a very common weed of hedgerows and other shady places. Also known as garlic mustard, it is native to Europe, Asia and north-western Africa but was probably introduced to North America as a culinary herb. It was first recorded as a wild plant on Long Island, New York in 1868 and has spread so persistently that it is now listed as a noxious weed in several states.

In European gardens it is not generally too much of a problem; it will seed generously if allowed but it does not spread by the root and is usually easy to pull out before the seed capsules open. The seeds contain around 15 per cent oil, mostly in the form of erucic acid, a monounsaturated fatty acid also found in rapeseed oil.

## Appearance and habitat

This is a member of the cabbage family (Brassicaceae), growing to around 70cm (2'4") tall. It has rich-green, roughly heart-shaped leaves which have wavy margins. The leaves smell distinctly but not intensely of garlic when crushed, giving rise to its alternative common name of garlic mustard. It is a biennial plant flowering in late spring with small, four-petalled, pure white flowers.

## Uses

Used as salad leaves and a green vegetable probably for thousands of years, recipes from the seventeenth century show that it was often used in sauces for fish and lamb. The leaves have a mild garlic taste with a hint of bitterness. However, prolonged cooking tends to destroy the garlic taste, leaving just the bitterness, so add the leaves towards the end of the cooking time when using them in recipes.

Use the leaves in place of basil to make pesto or make into soups and pasta sauces. They can be scattered over pizzas and included in quiches.

The long seedpods, if harvested when still green, can add crunch and flavour to salads or stir-fries. The roots are fairly chunky and work well in place of horseradish with vinegar, salt and sugar to make a mild version of horseradish sauce.

## Related plants

The annual honesty (*Lunaria annua*) can sometimes be a self-inflicted weed for gardeners. It is grown for the rich magenta-purple flowers and the seedpods that develop into translucent silvery discs, giving the plant the common name of silver dollars in the USA. There are white-flowered and variegated forms available. Once introduced to the garden, however, honesty can seed itself prolifically. If this is the case, you can eat both leaves and flowers in salads. The taproot can also be eaten as you would a radish – it has a similar spicy mustard taste.

## Jack's saag aloo

Serves 4
Approximate preparation time: 30 minutes

30g (1oz) butter

1 tbsp olive oil

5cm (2") piece ginger root, peeled and grated

2 onions, chopped

2 green or black chillies, chopped

200g (7oz) potatoes, peeled and diced

1 tsp ground cumin

1 tsp ground coriander

1 tsp turmeric

2 tbsp water or chicken stock

200g (7oz) Jack-by-the-hedge leaves, rinsed and chopped

Pinch of garam masala

1  Melt the butter and oil together in a large saucepan over a medium heat.

2  Fry the ginger, onions and chillies for 2 minutes, stirring frequently.

3  Add potatoes, cumin, coriander and turmeric and continue stirring for 5 minutes.

4  Add water or stock and cook gently for 15 minutes, or until potatoes are tender. Stir occasionally and add a little more water or stock if it starts to stick.

5  Add the chopped leaves, taking the saucepan off the heat after you've stirred them in. Sprinkle with garam masala and serve hot as a side dish.

# Japanese knotweed
## (*Fallopia japonica*)

A weed that strikes fear into the heart of any gardener, owing to its rampant and invasive nature, Japanese knotweed is nevertheless a very useful culinary plant. It is a good source of many essential minerals, particularly calcium, and contains large quantities of the plant polyphenol resveratrol, also present in grapes and berries. It has been shown to have antioxidant and anti-inflammatory effects.

## Appearance and habitat

Japanese knotweed was much praised in Victorian times for the bamboo-like stems, handsome heart-shaped leaves and fluffy white flowers. A herbaceous perennial, it produces annual stems that grow to 2-3m (6'6"-10') or more, from rhizomes that can go as much as 3m (10') deep. Once established it proves to be extremely invasive and very difficult to eradicate. It has spread along roadsides, railway banks and riverbanks and on wasteland. Even small fragments of root are able to regenerate into plants.

## Control

A native of Japan, Taiwan and northern China, Japanese knotweed was introduced to many other countries as an ornamental garden plant but is now a very invasive weed. Neither chemical nor mechanical methods are easy solutions for the long-term control of Japanese knotweed, and considerable resources are employed in trying to eliminate it. Specialist contractors had to be brought into the Olympic Park site in East London in 2007 as it was badly contaminated with the plant. Nearly 140,000 tonnes (138,000 tons) of contaminated soil were cleaned in situ. There are now strict regulations about taking Japanese knotweed to landfill sites as it is classed as controlled waste.

Domestic control is difficult, as digging out the deep rhizomes is a major undertaking. Systemic herbicides such as glyphosate can be used when the plant is in full leaf but not yet flowering. However, vigilance is required, with repeated applications necessary if regrowth occurs. Experiments are ongoing to see if it can be effectively controlled by an aphid-like psyllid, which feeds only on Japanese knotweed and the closely related giant knotweed.

## Uses

Young shoots and leaves are commonly eaten in Japan, and the edible properties of the plant are becoming more widely known as people realise that eating it is an effective and eco-friendly way of keeping the plant under control.[14] Knotweed has a tart, tangy taste, something like that of its relative rhubarb, and like rhubarb it can be used in both sweet and savoury recipes and combines well with ginger. It tends to be less stringy than rhubarb so works well in fools and sorbets.

The shoots are best harvested in early spring when they are around 15-20cm (6-8") tall. Once they have started to branch they are generally too tough to be useful. Chop into short lengths and boil or steam for just a few minutes until tender. Serve with melted butter or a Hollandaise sauce. If you have more knotweed than you can reasonably eat, you can blanch or freeze it for use later in the year.

Use in any recipes that you have for rhubarb such as fools, crumbles and tarts. Sweet preserves such as jams and marmalades are ideal for using up large quantities of knotweed, but it can also make tangy pickles and relishes. Cooked until they have gone mushy, the stems make an interesting tart sauce for oily fish such as mackerel. Make a sweet purée by gently simmering one cup of sugar to every four cups of chopped stems with a splash of orange juice. This is delicious spooned over halved strawberries.

The stems can be used to make an interesting wine of a beautiful tawny-gold colour. Freezing the knotweed then thawing it is the easiest way to release the juices for winemaking.

## Related species

Giant knotweed (*Fallopia sachalinensis*) is a similar plant but can grow even taller. Hybrids between the two species have occurred from time to time. *F. convolvulus* is the straggly black bindweed that occurs as a common annual weed in arable fields and gardens. Seeds of this plant were used as a food as far back as the Bronze Age and formed part of the last meal of Tollund Man.

CAUTION: Knotweed should not be eaten to excess due to the oxalic acid content.

Black bindweed sprawls along the ground.

## Easy knotweed soup

Serves 4
Approximate preparation time: 15 minutes

800g (1lb 12oz) young knotweed shoots, cut into short lengths

1 litre (35fl oz / 1¾ pints) vegetable or chicken stock

200g (7oz) cream cheese

1  Put the knotweed shoots into a saucepan and bring to the boil with the stock.

2  Simmer for 5-10 minutes then stir in the cream cheese and serve.

## Knotweed and orange marmalade

Approximate preparation time: 2-3 hours

4 oranges

4 cups knotweed shoots, cut into short lengths

400g (14oz) sugar

1  Peel the oranges, removing as much of the white pith as possible.

2  Slice the pulp and add to a preserving pan with the knotweed and a cup of water. Add the rind of two of the oranges, cut into thin strips.

3  Bring to the boil and simmer for an hour or so until the rind is tender.

4  Add the sugar, stirring until dissolved, then boil rapidly for 15-30 minutes until setting point is reached. Pour into sterile jars and seal.

## Knotweed tart

Serves about 6
Approximate preparation time: 1 hour

400g (14oz) young Japanese knotweed
shoots, cut into bite-sized lengths

200g (7oz) pastry

150g (5½oz) brown or demerara sugar

4 tbsp plain flour

2 eggs

4 tbsp cream

1  Parboil the knotweed shoots for a
minute or two, then drain.

2  Use the pastry to line a 20-22cm
(8-9") flan case.

3  Mix the sugar with flour, eggs and
cream to make a paste.

4  Fill the pastry case with the knotweed
then spread the paste over the top.
Bake in a hot oven (220°C / 425°F /
Gas Mark 7) for 10 minutes, then lower
the heat and cook for another 20
minutes.

## Knotweed in yogurt sauce

Serves 4 as a starter
Approximate preparation time: 20 minutes

200g (7oz) knotweed stems, trimmed
into pieces 10cm (4") long

1 tsp olive oil, plus olive oil for tossing

1 clove garlic

Salt and pepper

2 tsp sesame seeds

1 lemon, quartered

*For the sauce*

1 clove garlic

1 heaped tbsp tahini

Small pot full-fat yogurt

1  Simmer the knotweed in water with
1 tsp olive oil and one clove of garlic for
4-5 minutes until the stems are tender.

2  Drain in a colander for a few minutes,
then toss in olive oil and season with
salt and pepper.

3  To make the yogurt sauce, pound the
other garlic clove in a mortar until
mushy. Add the tahini and yogurt and
work until smooth.

4  Toast the sesame seeds in a pan
over a medium heat for a few minutes
until they begin to smell fragrant.

To serve, set the stems on individual
plates, add a spoonful of the sauce, the
sesame seeds, and a wedge of lemon.

# Meadowsweet
## (*Filipendula ulmaria*)

In medieval times meadowsweet was used as a strewing herb and it is said that Queen Elizabeth I liked to have it on the floors of her bedchamber.

In 1897 chemists working for the German firm Bayer AG modified salicin from willow bark and meadowsweet to form the chemical acetylsalicylic acid, which had first been synthesised by the French chemist Charles Frederic Gerhardt. Bayer named its product aspirin, after *Spiraea ulmaria*, which at that time was the botanical name for meadowsweet. Aspirin went on to become the world's most commercially successful drug. Meadowsweet is a good source of many antioxidant chemicals including flavonoids and vitamin C.

## Appearance and habitat

A herbaceous perennial with airy clouds of flowers like whipped cream may seem to be an unlikely member of the rose family, but meadowsweet, like geums and the strawberry, is indeed in the Rosaceae. It is common through most of Europe and western Asia and has naturalised in North America, growing in marshy land and damp woodland, often forming dense colonies along ditches. It grows to 1m (3') or more tall with attractive foliage that is dark green on the upper surface and whitish underneath.

The fluffy, cream-coloured flowers appear from June to September and are very attractive to insects. They have a rich sweet fragrance and were historically used to flavour mead.

## Uses

Meadowsweet has traditionally been used as an anti-inflammatory agent and as a herbal remedy for colds and fever. It is also used in pot pourri, as it retains its fragrance well on drying.

Strip individual leaflets from their stalks and add them to salads or infuse in boiling water to make a herbal tea.

The flowers are used to make an aromatic cordial, popular in Estonia, where it is known as *angervaksajook.*

The flowers, leaves and stems can be used to make a blue dye; a black dye is obtained from the roots.

## Related species

Dropwort, *Filipendula vulgaris*, differs from meadowsweet in its smaller size and more delicate, lacy leaves. It usually flowers about a month earlier and is more likely to be found on dry calcareous grassland. The North American species *F. rubra* can be as much as 2.5m (8') tall, with flowers that vary from deep peach to rose-pink in colour. It is commonly known as the Queen of the Prairie.

**CAUTION: Meadowsweet contains the fragrant chemical coumarin, high doses of which have caused liver problems in animal studies, so it should be used with caution.**

**Some people with asthma can be sensitive to aspirin; if so they would also need to avoid meadowsweet.**

## Meadowsweet cordial

Approximate preparation time: 1 hour, plus time to infuse

1¾ litres (60fl oz / 3 pints) water
Bucket or trugful of meadowsweet flowerheads
3 lemons, quartered
450g (1lb) sugar
50g (1¾oz) citric acid

1  Put the water into a large saucepan. Add the flowers and lemons and bring to the boil.

2  Turn off the heat and leave to infuse for a couple of hours. Strain through muslin then return the liquid to the pan and add sugar.

3  Bring to the boil again, stirring until the sugar has dissolved. Turn off the heat and stir in the citric acid. Pour into sterile bottles and seal. Serve diluted with water to taste.

# Meadowsweet dessert with cherry sauce

Serves 4
Approximate preparation time: 2 hours

3 leaves gelatine
250ml (9fl oz) milk
250ml (9fl oz) double cream
8 meadowsweet flowerheads
30g (1oz) sugar

*For the cherry sauce:*
150g (5½oz) sugar
150ml (5½fl oz) water
1 tbsp cherry liqueur
200g (7oz) cherries, de-stoned

1  Soak the gelatine leaves in a little cold water until soft.

2  Place the milk, cream, meadowsweet and sugar into a pan and bring to a simmer. Strain through a sieve and discard the flowerheads.

3  Squeeze the water out of the gelatine leaves, then add to the milk and cream mixture. Stir until the gelatine has dissolved.

4  Divide the mixture between four ramekins and leave to cool. Place into the fridge for at least an hour, until set.

5  To make the sauce, place the sugar, water and cherry liqueur into a pan and bring to the boil. Reduce the heat and simmer until the sugar has dissolved.

6  Take the pan off the heat and add all but a dozen cherries. Using a hand blender, blend the sauce until smooth.

To serve, turn each ramekin out on to a serving plate. Spoon over the sauce and garnish with reserved cherries.

# Mint
## (*Mentha* spp.)

places. The standard advice is to grow mint in pots or a large plastic container, but you do still need to ensure that the roots do not creep out of the bottom of the pots to start colonising the surrounding area. Mints are probably safest grown in wall or hanging baskets.

Mint was originally used as a medicinal herb, particularly to treat stomach conditions. It is still widely used today for digestive disorders. The Roman poet Ovid described an elderly couple scouring their table with mint to give it a pleasant scent in honour of their guests.

Mint is often a self-inflicted weed in the garden. Planted as a useful herb for its aromatic leaves, the creeping stoloniferous roots can spread quickly, infiltrating borders and even travelling under paths. They particularly flourish in moist, shady

Mints contain reasonable amounts of many minerals including iron and calcium, but are probably not eaten in large enough quantities to make a significant contribution to the diet.

## Appearance and habitat

Along with many other herbs, mints are in the family Lamiaceae. They have the characteristic square stem that is common to the family and are usually perennial plants. There are many different wild species and a large number of cultivated forms which can hybridise with wild species,

making it quite difficult to identify individual plants. The most commonly grown in gardens is spearmint (*Mentha spicata*), named for its pointed leaves. It has a fresh clean taste. Apple mint (*M. suaveolens*) has slightly woolly, rounded leaves and a richer flavour. Peppermint (*M. × piperita*) is widely cultivated for its essential oil, which is used medicinally as well as for

for culinary purposes. Water mint (*M. aquatica*) is common in the wild, being found particularly in ditches and at pond edges. Its taste is somewhat bitter compared with many of the cultivated varieties, so add rather more sugar if using this species in sauces.

## Uses

The leaves are used to flavour new potatoes and peas, and classically with roast lamb. In Britain they are usually made into a sauce, whereas in America mint jelly is more common.

Mint teas are traditionally made with the field mint *M. arvensis*. They are made by steeping the leaves in hot water for around 5 minutes and are commonly served in Middle Eastern countries. The leaves are also used as a garnish in other drinks such as fruit punches, the mint julep and mojito, and of course are essential to the liqueur crème de menthe.

The Middle East is also the home of tabbouleh, a Levantine salad composed of bulgar wheat, cucumber and tomato, flavoured with parsley and mint. Tzatziki is a classic Greek appetiser of strained yogurt and cucumber, usually made with added garlic and mint.

## Mint jelly

Makes about 3 jars
Approximate preparation time: 1 hour

570ml (20fl oz / 1 pint) apple juice
285ml (10fl oz / ½ pint) vinegar
1 sachet of pectin
1kg (2lb 3oz) sugar
Knob of butter
3 tbsp mint, finely chopped

1  Place the apple juice and vinegar in a large pan. Bring to the boil then remove from the heat.

2  Whisk in the pectin, then stir in the sugar. Heat gently while stirring until the sugar and pectin have dissolved.

3  Add the knob of butter, then – still stirring – increase the heat and bring to a full rolling boil. Boil for 4 minutes.

4  Remove from the heat and stir in the mint. Allow to cool for about 10 minutes, stirring occasionally, until the mint no longer floats on the surface. Pot into sterile glass jars and seal.

# Navelwort
## (*Umbilicus rupestris*)

A common plant on rock crevices and walls, navelwort is so named as the round leaves have a dimple in the centre, where the stem joins the leaf. so they resemble belly buttons. It is sometimes called wall pennywort, and was known by the Scottish botanist John Claudius Loudon (1783-1843) as navelwort spinach, as it was used as a spinach substitute.

## Appearance and habitat

Navelwort prefers acid soils and moist environments and in Britain it is more common in the west and in Scotland. It is a member of the Crassula family (Crassulaceae), which includes many succulent plants. It is a short-lived perennial plant flowering from May to August, with spikes of small green or creamy-coloured bells that grow to about 25cm (10") tall. Some plants have progressively smaller leaves up the flower stem. The leaves usually die back after flowering, but a fresh flush of growth occurs in late autumn or winter.

## Uses

The mild-flavoured fleshy leaves add an appealing crispness to salads, or can be used instead of cucumber in sandwiches. They make an attractive garnish for a range of foods and are excellent added to stir-fries. Leaves that are harvested when the plant is in flower usually have a stronger, less pleasant taste.

They were formerly used to soothe burns in the same way that the sap of *Aloe vera* is now used.

# Nipplewort
## (*Lapsana communis*)

The common name nipplewort is often said to derive from the resemblance of the flower buds to nipples, presumably to someone unfamiliar with anatomy. In fact, it was given that name by the English herbalist John Parkinson (1567-1650) as he was told that in Prussia it was named *papillaris* and was used to heal ulcers on women's nipples. The young leaves of nipplewort are a rich source of antioxidant flavonols and flavones.

## Appearance and habitat

A common annual weed of arable crops, hedgerows, roadsides and gardens, nipplewort seems able to germinate in virtually any season. The young plants form rosettes of light green leaves, and develop into quite tall branching plants to around 75cm (2'6") high. A member of the daisy family (Asteraceae), nipplewort is native to Europe and northern Asia but also grows as a weed in North America, Australia and New Zealand. It is sometimes known as dock cress, although it is neither a dock nor a cress.

The small yellow flowers look like miniature dandelions. On sunny days they open for only a few hours in the morning. The seeds do not have the plumes of hair that dandelions have; rather, they are contained within small pods. Leaves are sometimes infected with the rust fungus known as *Puccinia lapsance*.

## Uses

The young leaves can be eaten in salads or cooked like spinach. They can be slightly bitter when raw but the bitterness tends to disappear on cooking. Vigorous plants can be a useful source of spring greens. However, by the time that the plants start to send up flower stems, they are more likely to become somewhat chewy and bitter. The little flowers can brighten up green salads.

# Opposite-leaved golden saxifrage
## (*Chrysosplenium oppositifolium*)

In 1829 the Scottish botanist John Claudius Loudon reported that in the Vosges Mountains of eastern France the leaves of the golden saxifrage "are used copiously as a salad". Care must be taken not to confuse the plant with any of the weedy spurges (*Euphorbia* spp.), which look superficially similar.

## Appearance and habitat

This plant has a name that is rather bigger than it is. It is a dainty species that creeps along the ground, forming mats of rounded leaves held on square stems. A native of western and central Europe, it grows in moist soil in woods and along streams. It prefers acid soils and is usually found in shady sites. It is an indicator plant for ancient woodland and rarely a troublesome weed, although if conditions are to its liking it can spread by rooting stems to form extensive carpets. The flowers open in March through to May and are modest creations with no petals but yellowish-green bracts.

## Uses

The leaves have a crisp, succulent texture and a mild taste with just a slight hint of bitterness. They are generally used in salads but are good in egg sandwiches. They can also be cooked briefly with other spring greens such as chickweed and spring beauty, which grow in similar places.

## Related plants

Creeping saxifrage (*Saxifraga stolonifera*) is a garden flower with attractive rounded leaves and airy spires of white flowers. It is still sometimes eaten in Japan, either in salads or cooked.

# Oxeye daisy
## (*Leucanthemum vulgare*)

In ancient times daisies were dedicated to the moon goddess Isis and were used in love potions. There is perhaps a fragile echo of this heard when girls count the petals while whispering "He loves me, he loves me not." In Celtic legend daisies were said to be the spirits of children who had died during birth, which, given their prolific flowering, gives a worrying indication of birth survival rates at the time. During the Middle Ages daisies were reputed to be able to cure smallpox and madness. Oxeye daisies grow on a range of soils ranging from nutrient-rich clays to poor sandy soils. The nutritional quality of the plant is likely to depend on the growing medium.

## Appearance and habitat

A common and decorative plant of meadows, roadsides and hedgerows, tolerating dry conditions, the oxeye or moon daisy is found throughout Europe and much of Asia. In the USA it is considered to be a noxious weed in several states. It grows to 60-70cm (2'-2'4") tall, spreading by creeping rhizomes to form dense patches. The leaves are a rich, dark green and it has cheerful daisy flowers between May and August. It is a popular plant to grow in meadow-type borders, giving a pleasing informality to plantings.

## Uses

Early in spring the young shoots can be harvested. They are sometimes eaten raw in salads but have a bitter, pungent taste which is not popular. Soaking the shoots in salt water for 1 hour before rinsing and boiling them for 5-10 minutes makes them more acceptable. Alternatively, blanch the shoots under an upturned bucket for

7-10 days before harvesting. They can then be blanched and served with a vinaigrette dressing.

The flowers can be used to decorate mixed salads but again have quite a bitter taste, so use them sparingly. The unopened flower buds can be pickled and used as capers. They add a tang to pizzas or can be chopped and used in sauces for fish or chicken.

The lawn daisy.

## Related plants

It has long been recognised to be a sure sign of spring if you can stand on nine daisies with one foot. The common lawn daisy (*Bellis perennis*) can grow in great profusion, hugging the ground with its leaves so tightly that the lawn mower does no serious damage to the plant. The flowers are often used by children for making daisy chains, but are also edible. They have quite an astringent taste so you are unlikely to want to eat them regularly, but making daisy bud 'capers' is a useful alternative summer holiday activity for children.

## Pickled daisy buds

Approximate preparation time: 30 minutes, plus time to mature

2 mugfuls unopened daisy buds (either oxeye or lawn daisies)

6 black peppercorns

Pinch of salt

1 tsp mustard seeds

1 clove garlic, crushed

570ml (20fl oz / 1 pint) white wine vinegar

1  Pack the daisy buds into glass jars.

2  Put the other ingredients into a pan and bring to the boil. Take off the heat and allow to cool slightly before pouring into the jars, filling them to the brim.

3  Secure with vinegar-proof lids and leave to mature in a cool, dark place for 8 weeks before using.

# Pigweed
## (*Amaranthus retroflexus*)

In its native America pigweed, or amaranth, has been grown for its grain-like seeds since the time of the Aztecs. The seeds were used in an ancient ceremony in which they were mixed with beeswax and human blood and moulded into the shape of a man before being shared among the worshippers. The Spanish conquistador Cortéz halted the ritual and outlawed the cultivation of the amaranth crop. Amaranths are nutritious vegetables; a cup of boiled amaranth leaves can provide more than 50mg of vitamin C and nearly 3mg of iron.

## Appearance and habitat

This is a North American species which has naturalised widely in many other regions of the world. It is an annual plant with erect stout stems and pale green, stalked leaves that are oval to diamond-shaped. The leaves often turn red in autumn. In favourable conditions it can grow to as much as 3m (10') tall. Tiny hairs on the stems can irritate the skin so it is best to wear gloves if hand-weeding. The numerous flowers, borne in branched spikes, are greenish-white, and it flowers from June to October. It is a relative of the ornamental cockscomb and celosias, which are half-hardy plants grown for their showy plumes of flowers.

## Uses

The leaves can be gathered at any time. They stay fresh and edible through the summer. Young leaves are eaten raw in salads, whereas those from mature plants are best boiled as spinach.

In the Indian state of Kerala the plant is known as *cheera* and is one of the vegetables that can be used with coconut and chillies to make a popular vegetable dish called *thoran*. It provides a useful source of iron for vegetarians.

In Jamaica amaranth is called callaloo. It is usually soaked in salted water then rinsed and cooked with chillies, tomatoes and onions and often eaten as a breakfast dish. It differs from the callaloo of Trinidad, which is a thick soup that usually contains okra and taro.

The seeds can be sprinkled over home-made breads or added to seed cakes.

## Related species

Amaranths are a somewhat confusing group of plants, and it often requires microscopic examination of the fruit to distinguish between the species. The ornamental Prince-of-Wales feather plant delights in the scientific name of *Amaranthus hypochondriacus*. It originates in Mexico but is used as a food plant in parts of Africa. The seeds contain more protein than cereals such as wheat and rice and so there is a burgeoning interest in their use in many areas of the world, particularly as the plants are tolerant of drought. They are eaten as a snack food in Mexico City, sometimes mixed with chocolate. Many amaranths have been bred for colour and their spinach-like flavour. They are ideal for use as baby-leaf salad crops.

**CAUTION: Amaranth leaves contain oxalic acid so should not be eaten to excess.**

## Pigweed thoran

Served as a side dish
Approximate preparation time: 15 minutes

1 tsp mustard seeds

2 tbsp olive oil

2 generous handfuls of pigweed leaves, chopped

3 tbsp coconut, grated

2 cloves garlic

1 large onion, chopped

3 green chillies, de-seeded and chopped

½ tsp cumin powder

1 tsp turmeric

1 Fry the mustard seeds in the oil.

2 Add the pigweed and allow to cook for a couple of minutes.

3 Crush together the coconut, garlic, onion, chillies and spices, then add to the pan.

4 Mix well and cook for a further 5 minutes. Serve as a side dish with rice.

# Pineapple weed
## (*Matricaria discoidea*)

Pineapple weed has long been used in its native America as a worming agent and remedy for digestive disorders, but it has culinary as well as medicinal properties. The leaves and flowers have a high lipid content and its oils give the plant its characteristic fragrance.

## Appearance and habitat

Pineapple weed is a short, somewhat sprawling annual plant with attractive, deep-green feathery leaves. It is distinguished from other mayweeds by the lack of white petals and a definite pineapple aroma. It is native to North America and north-east Asia. In Britain it is said to have escaped from Kew Gardens in the late nineteenth century and is now found throughout the country on fertile, disturbed ground. Like plantains, it is tolerant of trampling, so is often found on paths and in gateways. Seeds can be distributed on the tyres of cars. A single plant can produce thousands of seeds so hand-weeding or hoeing young plants before they start to flower is recommended.

## Uses

Both flowerheads and leaves can be used raw in salads or nibbled on as a snack while out walking. However, while they do have a pineapple taste, they also have an underlying bitterness, which means they are not best eaten on their own. The flowerheads, though, add interest when scattered over a mixed salad, preferably one including stronger flavours such as the lemon tang of sorrel, or with a good balsamic vinegar dressing.

## Related species

Scented mayweed (*Matricaria recutita*), also known as wild chamomile, is sometimes used in herbal teas as a substitute for the true chamomile.

# Plantain
## (*Plantago* spp.)

Plantains are renowned for having powerful coagulant properties and the common plantain was used on battle-fields as a wound dressing. In Shakespeare's *Romeo and Juliet*, Romeo ironically suggests that a plantain leaf will cure a broken shin. In North America the greater or rat-tail plantain (*Plantago major*) is known as white-man's foot because plants have grown wherever the European settlers travelled. The seeds are easily carried on the soles of shoes and were a common contaminant in cereal grains that the settlers took with them.

Seeds of *Plantago ovata* have been shown to contain 17.4 per cent protein of a high biological value. They are also a good source of linoleic acid, which is an essential fatty acid in the human diet.

## Appearance and habitat

There are some 200 species of plantains, which are distributed all over the world. The common name can cause confusion with the fruit plantain, a type of banana much used in West Indian cuisine. However, plantains of the genus *Plantago* are mostly familiar and persistent weeds with low-growing rosettes of leaves and stalked spikes of grain-like flowers. Some of the alpine species are grown on rock gardens for their ornamental silvery leaves, and there are horticultural selections of other species grown in gardens.

A natural mutation of the common plantain, *P. major* 'Rosularis', known since the sixteenth century, has whorls of small spoon-shaped bracts, so the flowers look like small green roses. This form is also known as 'Bowles's Variety' after the famous horticulturalist E. A. Bowles. He grew it at Myddelton House in Middlesex, in an area of garden he called his 'Lunatic Asylum' as it included other bizarre plants such as the corkscrew hazel and Plymouth strawberry. There is also a form of *P. major* called 'Rubrifolia', which is valued for its deep bronze-purple colouration.

Plantain leaves are extremely tough and resilient, showing great tolerance of mowing and trampling, so plantains are often found growing on paths where few other weeds survive. The ribwort plantain, *P. lanceolata*, which has lance-shaped leaves and shorter, darker flowerheads, is rather less resilient and more likely to be found at the edge of paths. This species has also been introduced to the Americas and Australia, where it is considered an invasive weed. In the garden, plantains are usually easily hand pulled or forked out, so long as the soil is reasonably moist.

## Uses

The young leaves of plantains are often said to be edible raw; they are extremely tough and chewy, though, and do not really make good eating. It is noticeable in my garden that the wild rabbits will feast on my hosta leaves and totally ignore the plantains growing next to them. I tend to agree with them, as young hosta shoots are delicious, whereas I find that plantains have an odd taste. This is sometimes described as a mushroom flavour but reminds me more of washing powder. Mature leaves contain long, stringy fibres similar to those in celery stalks. If you want to cook them, first cut them across the leaf to cut through the fibres, then boil or steam as you would cabbage.

Ribwort plantain has a better texture and taste than that of the common plantain. Try the leaves dipped in tempura batter and deep fried. The flower spikes can be blanched and served with a vinaigrette dressing.

Today it is the husks of species such as *P. ovata* and *P. afra* (syn. *P. psyllium*) that are most commonly used. These contain a mucilaginous dietary fibre and, when taken with plenty of fluid, are effective at relieving constipation and possibly useful in treating irritable bowel disease. They are sold commercially as psyllium seed husks and can be used in gluten-free baking to make breads less crumbly. Studies indicate that they may be of benefit in reducing the risk of heart disease. A Mexican placebo-controlled trial on people with diabetes found significant improvements in blood glucose and lipid levels after using psyllium for 6 weeks.[15]

> **CAUTION: There have been suggestions that plantains could interfere with absorption of warfarin and other anticoagulants, and so people taking such medicines should not eat plantains.**

# Purslane
## (*Portulaca oleracea*)

Purslane is native from North Africa through to India and in Australasia, but was introduced to Britain in medieval times, when it was used as a salad vegetable and in pickles. European settlers took it to North America, where it is now considered to be a weed. Purslane is considered to be an important food in China and India and was described in Chinese medical literature around AD 500. It is regularly sold in French markets during the summer, under the name *pourpier*. It is one of the main ingredients in the Levantine bread salad *fattoush*.

Purslane is unusual among vegetables in that it is a relatively rich source of omega-3 fatty acids, normally thought to be found in significant amounts only in oily fish and flax seeds.[16] Omega-3 fatty acids are considered to be protective against heart disease.

## Appearance and habitat

Purslane is a low-growing plant with reddish brittle stems, any broken bits of which may root to form new plants. It has glossy green, plump, succulent leaves that form a cluster at the stem tips. The small, pale yellow flowers open for just a few hours in the morning. The small seedpods held tight against the stems are unusual and look like tiny cups with an elf's cap cover, which drops off to reveal the black seeds.

There are a number of different cultivars including a paler-leaved form (said to be golden, but more of a yellowish-green) in cultivation around the world. Purslane evolved in hot, dry climates and is drought-tolerant, so is a useful plant for the water-wise gardener. Plants are frost tender and quickly die back in winter. Unwanted plants are easily pulled by hand or can be removed with a hoe, but any pieces left on the ground (or on the top of a compost heap) may quickly re-root.

## Uses

The stems, leaves and flowers are all edible and have a refreshing, tangy flavour with a slight saltiness. Plants have a higher acid content first thing in the morning so if you have a sweet tooth, harvest after a sunny day to eat for your supper. It can be eaten raw in salads or cooked as spinach. It has a mucilaginous, somewhat slimy quality when cooked, which some people find off-putting. However, this does make it useful as a thickener in soups and stews.

**CAUTION: Unfortunately purslane is high in oxalic acid so you should not eat excessive quantities of it.**

### Purslane à la française

Serves about 4
Approximate preparation time: 20 minutes

1 onion, chopped

1 tbsp olive oil

1 large bunch purslane/*pourpier*, chopped

250ml (9fl oz) vegetable or chicken stock

100g (3½oz) peas

100g (3½oz) mange touts

100g (3½oz) broad beans

Handful of mint leaves, chopped

1  Fry the onion in oil until soft.

2  Add the purslane to the onion and stir until just wilted.

3  Pour in the stock and add the other vegetables; simmer until everything is tender. Mix in the mint just before serving.

# Reedmace
(*Typha* spp.)

Archaeological evidence suggests that in Europe the edible rhizomes of reedmace (often called 'bulrush') were ground for flour as long as 30,000 years ago. In more recent times they have rarely been used as a food in Britain, but in rural America they are eaten fairly regularly, where they are often called Cossack asparagus. The rhizomes are a useful source of carbohydrate and the young leaf shoots are high in dietary fibre and vitamin K. In Nevada the Paiute people used the stems and leaves for building boats, and the yellow pollen was used both as a flour and medicinally as an anti-coagulant. The fluffy down was used to stuff pillows and line moccasins.

## Appearance and habitat

These are not the bulrushes of Moses: that is the species *Cyperus papyrus*, and indeed botanists encourage us to call *Typha* species 'reedmace' to distinguish them from the true bulrush. Known in America as cattails but in Britain and Australia as bulrushes, there are thought to be 11 species in the genus *Typha*, and all are found in wetland habitats. The common reedmace, *T. latifolia*, is the most widespread, and is an extremely vigorous plant, with leaves growing to 2.5m (8').

The numerous female flowers form a dense brown sausage-shaped structure on the stem, above which are the male flowers, which shed large quantities of yellow pollen. Plants usually flower in June and July and are wind-pollinated. Once the seeds are ripe the heads disintegrate into a mass of cottony fluff which blows away on the wind. It soon colonises areas of wet mud, and its dense growth crowds out other species. The cultivar 'Variegata' is rather slower growing, with leaves prominently striped in cream and green. It usually reaches around 1.2m (4') in height.

## Uses

The leaf bases can be eaten in early spring while they are still tender, when they have a fresh cucumber-like taste. Throughout spring and summer the stalks can be cut and the inner portion of the stem eaten. The outer covering of the stalk is removed by pulling down on the leaves that cover it. The succulent white inner part can then be washed and eaten raw, chopped up for salads, or cooked in a stew.

In early summer the sheath can be removed from the developing green flower spike, which can then be boiled for 5-10 minutes and eaten like corn on the cob. They are fiddly to eat, and somewhat chewy, but acceptable when eaten with plenty of butter.

The pollen can be harvested by bending over the stalk tips and shaking them into a paper bag. It has a sweet, slightly soapy taste. It can be used as a flour substitute, but on its own does not work in cakes and breads due to the lack of gluten. This quality does mean that it can be used by people with coeliac disease. Use one part pollen to two or three parts ordinary flour in recipes for biscuits, pancakes and muffins. The resulting products are an attractive yellowish colour. The underground rhizomes are usually harvested from late autumn to early spring. It is a fairly messy job to dig them out; then they must be rinsed and peeled to release the starchy flakes within. Ground and sifted, the rhizomes have been used to make flour, but on a domestic scale it is time-consuming. In spring, potato-like buds form on the rhizomes and these can be harvested and boiled, and served with melted butter or roasted.

The dried spikes are attractive in flower arrangements. You can spray them with hairspray to reduce the likelihood of the seedheads shattering and filling your home with fluff.

CAUTION: Be sure you can distinguish reedmace from the yellow iris *Iris pseudacorus*, which often grows alongside and has similar leaves. The iris is poisonous and can cause vomiting.

While the plants are undoubtedly of value in wildlife ponds, reedmace should be planted with caution. The rhizomes have very sharp tips and are capable of puncturing pond liners.

# Rose
## (*Rosa* spp.)

The simple five-petalled dog rose appears on many medieval heraldic shields and is an easily recognised and much-loved species as well as being a useful plant. In Britain in 1942 the Ministry of Health organised the collection of 400 tons (about 406 tonnes) of rose hips to be processed into the National Rose Hip Syrup, because of its high vitamin C content. This was sold at a low standard price for distribution to children.

A Norwegian investigation has shown that the hips are significantly higher in antioxidants than most so-called superberries. Hips of *Rosa canina* contain a total antioxidant content of 35.17 mmol/100g compared with levels of 7.57 mmol/100g for blueberries.[17]

## Appearance and habitat

There are many different wild roses growing throughout the world, the most common being dog roses (*Rosa canina* agg.). This variable group grows in hedgerows, thickets and at the edges of woodlands. They have long, arching stems armed with sharp thorns and single white or pink flowers in early summer, followed by scarlet sealing-wax coloured hips that can last on the plant well into winter. These familiar flowers are a regular feature in folklore and poetry. They are a popular nectar source for many insects and the leaves are eaten by mammals such as rabbits and deer. Field and dog roses are important for the lifecycle of the gall wasp. The bizarre-looking galls known as robin's pincushions develop as a chemically induced distortion of a leaf or terminal bud in which the larvae overwinter.

## Control

Sleeping Beauty's prince found that an impenetrable rose hedge burst into bloom and parted for him at a touch, but those of us without royal blood can find mature wild roses more difficult to control. Unwanted seedling plants are best removed as soon as you see them, because large plants are uncomfortable to deal with due to the aggressive nature of the thorns, which can be felt even through leather gloves. Cut the stems down in stages with secateurs or a pruning saw, then dig deeply with a spade to remove the entire root.

## Uses

The hips have a higher proportion of vitamin C than oranges and are still widely used for rosehip syrup, often using the same recipes that were recommended in wartime. The hairs that line the hips have been used by generations of children as an itching powder. If using rose hips at home for syrups or jellies, take care to strain out these prickly hairs by passing the liquid through double layers of muslin.

Rosehip purée is made by simmering the hips in water for 20 minutes then sieving them to remove the pips and hair. Boiling the pulp with half its weight of sugar for 10 minutes makes a delicious soft conserve to spread on bread or make into tarts.

Hips can be dried by spreading them on a baking tray and leaving in the sun. The dried hips are used to make a tea by crushing them with a rolling pin and infusing 1 teaspoonful per cup of boiling water. It has a sweet, astringent taste. In Sweden the dried pulp of rose hips is traditionally used to make a soup-like dessert.

Rose water is made by covering a bowl of rose petals with boiling water and leaving them to infuse overnight. The next day the water is strained through muslin or a tea towel, squeezing all the moisture from the petals. Pour it into sterile bottles. Use in your bath, to fragrance rice in Persian-style cuisine or coconut ice, or tie on a label with ribbon and give to someone you love.

The flower petals from most roses can be used in salads, but taste them first as some have a slightly bitter aftertaste. Crystallise them by brushing with beaten egg white then sprinkling with sugar, or use to make rose petal syrup or jelly. Rose petal jam is very popular in the Middle East, where it is often stirred into yogurt as a dessert.

## Related species

The eglantine of Shakespeare is sweetbriar (*Rosa rubiginosa*), which has sticky, apple-scented leaves. The tender young shoots of this species can be eaten in salads. The green leaves were commonly used in France to flavour liqueurs. Rugosa roses are coastal plants from eastern Asia. They are widely used as ornamental plants and as thorny hedgerow plants, but have also seeded themselves around in many regions. Their petals have a stronger flavour than those of dog roses. The large squat hips, sometimes called sea tomatoes, are particularly useful for preserves.

The hips of a rugosa rose.

## Rose petal jam

Approximate preparation time: 45 minutes

2 cups rose petals
2 cups sugar
Juice of 1 orange

**1** Put the ingredients in a saucepan with half a cup of water and stir over a very low heat for about half an hour until thickened and the petals have disintegrated.

**2** Pot into a sterile glass jar and seal.

## Bridesmaids' smoothie

Serves about 4
Approximate preparation time: 10 minutes

Half a watermelon, peeled, chopped and de-seeded

Generous handful of rose petals (or 100ml (3½fl oz) rose water)

200g (7oz) Greek yogurt

200g (7oz) strawberries

1 banana

1 tbsp honey

**1** Place all the ingredients in a blender and blitz until smooth. Add more honey if necessary.

# Rosebay willowherb
## (*Epilobium angustifolium*)

Rosebay willowherb was widely used by the Native American people. Dried leaves were used as a tea substitute in Russia.

Rosebay willowherb was uncommon in Britain before the expansion of the railway system in the nineteenth century opened up corridors by which the seeds, plumed with white hairs, could travel in the slipstream of trains. It grows best on fertile soils and in the USA is usually known as fireweed because it is one of the first pioneer species to colonise a site after forest fires. During the Second World War in England it sprang up among the ruins of buildings after the widespread bombings of 1940, and was referred to as Bombsite Bessie. The leaves are a good source of calcium and potassium as well as vitamins A and C. The flowers contain tannins, which are thought to have antioxidant properties, but in large quantities these can interfere with the absorption of minerals such as iron.

## Appearance and habitat

*Epilobium angustifolium* is the accepted name for the plant also known as *Chamaenerion angustifolium*. Native throughout the temperate regions of the northern hemisphere, it is a member of the family Onagraceae, which includes the evening primrose and the fuchsia.

Rosebay willowherb is a statuesque plant growing up to 2.5m (8') tall with spires of rosy-purple flowers. A white form is sometimes sold as an ornamental plant. The robust reddish stems have narrow willow-like leaves arranged in a spiral. It is the main food plant of the caterpillar of the elephant hawk-moth. It flowers from June to

September and is a useful nectar source for bees and moths. The thick, white, rhizomatous roots can expand by around 1m (3') a year, so the plant can soon form dense stands.

## Control

If you want to control it, the roots are relatively easy to dig out, but they can be quite brittle, so ensure that you remove any broken pieces. Alternatively, repeatedly cutting or pulling up the stems will weaken and kill the plant.

## Uses

Young shoots, cut when they first emerge in spring, can be eaten like asparagus or tossed into stir-fries. Harvest them when they are up to about 30cm (1') tall, cutting below soil level, as you would with asparagus. The underground portion, which has been blanched by the soil, is the sweetest part. You can also blanch shoots by inverting a bucket over them when they first start to show above the ground.

The fresh young leaves are eaten in salads or cooked as a vegetable, but they are quite astringent and leaves usually become too bitter by midsummer. Dried leaves can be used as a herbal tea.

The mature stems can be peeled and the starchy pith used to thicken soups and stews.

Great willowherb.

The flower buds and open blossoms look attractive scattered through salads or over cakes and desserts. In Alaska a sweet jelly is made from the petals in a similar way to making rose petal jam. It can be served with ham and other cold meats or on bread or waffles.

## Related species

The willowherb genus *Epilobium* includes more than 200 different species. There are unconfirmed reports of toxicity after eating great willowherb, *E. hirsutum*, so it would be sensible to avoid experimentation, although a recent Romanian study using animals found no cytotoxic effects.[18]

# Alaskan fireweed jelly

Makes 3-4 jars
Approximate preparation time: 1 hour

1 litre (35fl oz / 1¾ pints) rosebay willowherb petals

1 litre (35fl oz / 1¾ pints) water

2 lemons

1kg (2 lb 3oz) sugar

1  Put the petals and water into a pan, bring to the boil and simmer for 10 minutes.

2  Strain the liquid through muslin (or a tea towel) then return to the rinsed pan.

3  Squeeze the lemons and add the juice and any pips to the strained liquid. The pips have the highest concentration of pectin, which aids setting of the jelly.

4  Add the sugar and stir until dissolved. Return to the heat and boil until setting point is reached (approximately 10 minutes).

5  Remove the lemon pips, pour the jelly into sterile jars and seal.

# Rosebay scones

Makes 8 scones
Approximate preparation time: 30 minutes

1 tsp baking powder

200g (7oz) self-raising flour

50g (1¾oz) butter

50g (1¾oz) sugar

150ml (5½fl oz) sour cream

1 teacupful rosebay willowherb flowers

1  Stir the baking powder into the flour.

2  Rub in the butter.

3  Stir in sugar then spoon in the sour cream and mix to a firm dough. Turn out on to a floured surface and sprinkle the flowers over the dough.

4  Knead very gently just a few times to mix the flowers into the dough.

5  Pat into a rough circle about 2cm (just under 1") thick. Use a cutter to make into individual scones or score into eight pieces. Brush the tops with eggwash if desired. Bake in a hot oven (220°C / 425°F / Gas Mark 7) for about 12 minutes.

# Shepherd's purse
## (*Capsella bursa-pastoris*)

Shepherd's purse has been eaten for thousands of years. Seeds were found in the stomach of Tollund Man and during excavation of the Neolithic Çatalhöyük site in Turkey, which dates back to 5950 BC. The plant is high in antioxidants such as flavonoids. It also contains relatively high concentrations of omega-6 polyunsaturated fatty acids and vitamins A, C and K, particularly in young leaves. The iron content of raw leaves is around 3.5mg per 100g, which is almost as much as in spinach.

## Appearance and habitat

Shepherd's purse is a widespread and familiar annual weed, found on cultivated land or waste ground. It is a member of the brassica family (Brassicaceae), but has a less pungent taste than many of the mustards as it contains a smaller concentration of the sulphur-containing chemicals known as glucosinolates. It is native to Europe and Asia Minor, but has now spread widely throughout North America. It can grow in great abundance, although it is not too difficult to deal with as the taproot is thin and uproots easily. If the rosette of leaves is severed from its taproot with a hoe it should not grow back.

The first true leaves have a smooth outline but later leaves are deeply lobed with a greyish appearance. It has tiny white flowers which are followed by the heart-shaped seedpods much loved by children, who like to pull them apart to reveal the diminutive coins within. It can be found in flower in any month of the year and is normally self-pollinated, setting seed rapidly. The seeds can remain viable in the soil for several years.

## Uses

The young leaves have a fresh tangy flavour and make an interesting addition to salads. They are considered a delicacy in parts of China. On mature plants the leaves become rather tough but they can be cooked with mixed spring greens.

The decorative seedpods can be gathered easily by running your hands up the stem. They make an intriguing addition to the salad bowl or scattered as a garnish over tomato soup.

The roots can be scrubbed and eaten like a somewhat skinny radish. They taste fairly bland initially, but have a warmth that creeps up on you.

## Related plants

Pink shepherd's purse, *Capsella rubella*, originates from the Mediterranean region but has naturalised as far as Britain. Shepherd's cress (*Teesdalia nudicaulis*) is found particularly on acid, sandy soils and shingle at the coast. Its scientific name comes not from the Pennine valley Teesdale, but from Robert Teesdale, a Yorkshire botanist. It is a smaller, lower-growing plant than shepherd's purse and the seed capsules are more oval in shape.

---

### Sweetheart salad

Serves 2
Approximate preparation time:
10 minutes

200g (7oz) cherry tomatoes, halved (if you can get them, the cultivars 'Tondino di Manduira' and 'Tomato Berry' are often naturally heart-shaped)

100g (3½oz) strawberries, quartered

Handful of young shepherd's purse leaves, plus some seedpods

1 tbsp olive oil

1 tsp balsamic vinegar

1 tsp demerara sugar

30g (1oz) Parmesan cheese shavings

1  Mix the cherry tomatoes and the strawberries in a salad bowl with the leaves.

2  Mix the oil with the vinegar and sugar until the sugar has dissolved.

3  Pour the dressing over the salad, and scatter with cheese and seedpods.

# Silverweed
## (*Potentilla anserina*)

in his *Carmina Gadelica* that reports the use of silverweed tubers as winter nuts, eaten between the feast of St Andrew (30th November) and Christmas time. In Scotland silverweed was commonly known as *brisgean*, and the tubers were regularly used as a source of starch before the introduction of the potato. The specific name *anserina* means 'of the geese' and refers to the use of silverweed as goose fodder.

The generic name *Potentilla* comes from the Latin *potens*, meaning 'powerful', a reference to the alleged medicinal properties of plants in this genus. (Some taxonomists, however, put the plant in the genus *Argentina*.)

The folklorist Alexander Carmichael (1832-1912) recorded a Scottish rhyme

In the eighteenth century herbalists recommended placing the leaves of silverweed in your shoes to keep feet cool and prevent sweating. The plants are still used as a traditional foodstuff in parts of China.[19] A tea made from silverweed was supposedly helpful for women while giving birth, or as a cure for menstrual cramps, and it was also used to treat diarrhoea. The amino acid profile of silverweed tubers complements that of barley, and in Tibet the two foods are combined to make a complete protein food to help alleviate childhood malnutrition.

## Appearance and habitat

A widespread and common plant along roadsides, farm tracks and waste ground, silverweed is quite tolerant of trampling and so may be seen on paths and in gateways. In moist, fertile soils it may not seem particularly silvery, but in dry, sandy conditions it is a really beautiful plant with silvery fern-like leaves and small yellow flowers similar to buttercups. It is not a member of the buttercup family, though; instead, it is related to roses. It can be found throughout the temperate regions of the northern hemisphere.

It is a perennial plant spreading by runners like those of strawberry plants. It grows just 10-30cm (4-12") tall and makes a dense ground cover, flowering usually from June to August. The roots form small, hazelnut-sized tubers.

## Uses

The young shoots and silvery leaves are edible; they look lovely in a salad bowl but are extremely chewy and not really recommended as a part of your normal meals.

The root tubers can be eaten raw or served baked or boiled. They have a crisp texture and vaguely nutty flavour. If you harvest enough of them they can be dried and ground into flour for bread and thickening sauces, and would be suitable for someone on a gluten-free diet. They are, unfortunately, fairly labour-intensive to harvest and clean, so it is probably only worth the effort in times of famine or if you are totally overrun with the plant.

## Related species

Creeping cinquefoil, *Potentilla reptans*, is a smaller, weedy-looking plant with toothed leaves divided into five leaflets. These suggested its name, cinquefoil, which comes from the French for 'five leaves'. It flourishes in dry soil, and the invasive runners can grow to 1.5m (5') long in a season. Leaves and flowers of this plant were used in compresses to relieve rheumatism. Like silverweed it produces root tubers, but they are high in tannins so should not be eaten to excess.

# Sorrel
## (*Rumex acetosa*)

The name sorrel derives from the French word *surir*, meaning 'to sour', and refers to the sharp, acidic taste of the leaves. Sorrel leaves used to be eaten by field-workers as a way of quenching the thirst. Sorrels are often grown as perennial vegetables but can also turn up in gardens as weeds. Raw sorrel leaves contain around 48mg of vitamin C per 100g. They also contribute a number of minerals including iron, calcium and magnesium.

## Appearance and habitat

Sorrels are closely related to docks but are distinguished by their spear-shaped leaves, which have a distinct acid tang. Common sorrel is a perennial species with separate male and female plants flowering in May and June. It grows to around 80cm (2'8") tall and has downward-pointing leaf lobes. It is found widely on verges, riverbanks and clearings in woodland but dislikes very limy soils. Some forms turn an attractive beetroot-red colour as the weather gets colder in winter. The cultivar 'Abundance' is a non-flowering form so will not seed around in the garden.

## Uses

Pick the leaves as required through the year; in moist soils plants will crop steadily all season. The plants die back in winter but re-emerge very early in the spring. The sharp lemon flavour of sorrel leaves is delicious in salads, especially when combined with the peppery warmth of rocket.

Sorrel is particularly popular in France,
where it is used in many soups and
sauces. The classic *potage Germiny*
uses ribbons of sorrel, known as
*chiffonade*, moistened with chicken
stock and thickened with egg yolks.

The leaves are traditionally used in the
Greek savoury pastry known as
*spanakopita*, which is usually served at
Pentecost, the festival when Christians
celebrate the gift of the Holy Spirit.

Sorrel sauces contrast well with rich
fatty foods such as pork, oily fish or
baked salmon. Add some leaves to a
cream cheese filling for sandwiches
and bagels. They are delicious wilted
into omelettes just as the omelette is
about to set, or combined with a hot
potato salad. Sorrel can even be used
in sweet dishes in place of rhubarb
and gooseberries.

The juice from the leaves is sometimes
used to clean copper and is said to be
able to remove ink stains from linen.
Sorrels and docks are food plants for
the small copper butterfly.

## Related species

French or buckler sorrel (*Rumex
scutatus*) is native to central and
southern Europe, western Asia and
North Africa, where it is found sprawling over rocky cliffs and roadsides. It
has been introduced to many other
countries as a culinary herb. It grows
to around 45cm (1'6") tall and has
squat, shield-shaped leaves; smaller
than those of common sorrel with an
even more intense flavour. It is perfect
for adding with a knob of butter to
just-boiled new potatoes.

There is a very ornamental cultivar
known as 'Silver Shield', which has
leaves marbled with a soft silver
colouration. It makes an attractive
ground-cover plant but can be somewhat rampant.

French sorrel has small leaves.

Sheep's sorrel, *R. acetosella*, is a characteristic plant of heathland and grassland on acid, sandy soils. It is a lower-growing plant to around 25cm (10") with leaves that have basal lobes spreading outwards. It flowers from May to September. The leaves have a wonderful lemony tang.

## Apple and sorrel sorbet

Serves about 4
Very approximate preparation time: 2 hours

100g (3½ oz) sugar
150ml (5½fl oz) water
400g (14oz) apples, peeled and chopped
Handful of sorrel leaves
1 egg white

1  Wash and chop the sorrel leaves and put them in a pan with the sugar, water and apples. Bring to the boil and boil for 5 minutes.

2  Allow to cool and then mix in a blender until smooth.

3  Pour into a plastic container and freeze for an hour.

4  Beat the egg white until stiff, then fold into the apple mixture. Return to the freezer until time to serve.

## French sorrel soup

Serves 4-6
Approximate preparation time: 40 minutes

1 onion, chopped
30g (1oz) butter
200g (7oz) sorrel leaves
1 small round lettuce
1 litre (35fl oz / 1¾ pints) chicken or vegetable stock
2 large egg yolks
1 tbsp cream
2 tbsp croutons

1  Sweat the onion in butter for 5-10 minutes.

2  Wash and chop the sorrel and lettuce. Add to the onion and allow to wilt.

3  Pour on the stock and simmer for 15 minutes.

4  Sieve through a metal sieve. Return soup to pan and heat gently.

5  Beat the egg yolks in a bowl with a few tablespoons of soup.

6  Pour the egg mixture into the pan and stir over a low heat until slightly thickened. Serve with a spoonful of cream and a scattering of croutons.

## Sorrel pasties

Serves about 4
Approximate preparation time: 40 minutes

400g (14oz) shortcrust pastry

Handful of sorrel leaves

Demerara sugar

Eggwash

1  Roll out the pastry thinly and cut into saucer-sized rounds.

2  Wash and chop the sorrel leaves and put a little heap on half of each round of pastry.

3  Sprinkle with sugar and fold the pastry over.

4  Brush with eggwash and bake in a hot oven (220°C / 425°F / Gas Mark 7) for around 20 minutes until golden. Serve with a spoonful of good vanilla ice cream or use as picnic food.

## Spanakopita

Serves about 4
Approximate preparation time: 1 hour

1kg (2lb 3oz) mixed green leaves, including sorrel and spinach

Salt

4 spring onions, chopped

Handful of parsley, chopped

Handful of dill, chopped

Handful of mint, chopped

Ground black pepper

4 tbsp olive oil

200g (7oz) filo pastry (about 24 sheets)

1  Wash the greens, roughly chop them and place in a colander.

2  Sprinkle with salt and allow to drain for 10 minutes, rinse, then press or squeeze to remove the excess liquid.

3  Combine the greens with the onions, herbs, pepper and 2 tbsp oil and mix well.

4  Brush a 22cm (9") round spring-form tin with oil.

5  Lay half the filo sheets in the tin, overlapping them and brushing each one lightly with olive oil.

6  Spoon in the greens mixture and spread evenly, folding the filo over the edges.

7  Cover with the remaining filo, brushing each with oil. Brush the top with oil and lightly splash with water.

8  Bake in a medium oven (180°C / 350°F / Gas Mark 4) for half an hour until golden brown. You can add 2 eggs and 200g (7oz) feta cheese to the greens mixture for a more substantial pie.

# Sow-thistle
## (*Sonchus* spp.)

Not, it must be said, the most appetising-looking of plants, sow-thistles (as the common name suggests) can be prickly and presumably only thought worth feeding to pigs. However, for those who do not like their food too bland, they can be surprisingly good eating. Sow-thistles are high in dietary fibre and contain more protein and lipids than cultivated green vegetables such as cabbage. They are high in antioxidants including vitamin C.

## Appearance and habitat

The most common of the many species are prickly sow-thistle (*Sonchus asper*), smooth sow-thistle (*S. oleraceus*) and perennial sow-thistle (*S. arvensis*). These are found on waste ground and any regularly disturbed land. The flowers are dandelion-like and turn into fluffy seedheads.

The smooth and prickly sow-thistles are similar-looking annual species and can hybridise. They grow to around 1m (3') or more and have hollow stems which leak a milky sap if broken. Perennial sow-thistle has larger flowers, with orange-coloured hairs on the receptacle and flowering stem. It can grow to around 1.5m (5') high.

### Control

If left to seed sow-thistles will spread throughout the garden, but they are fairly easy to hand pull or hoe out.

Even the prickly species is not as aggressive as true thistles.

## Uses

Young leaves of sow-thistles can be eaten raw. Seedlings are quite mild, but as they age they become more bitter. Blanching young plants under a bucket for a few days reduces the bitterness. Mature leaves will need to have any prickles cut off with kitchen scissors. They are best soaked in salted water for 1 hour, then rinsed before boiling for 5 minutes, and can then be eaten as a green vegetable or incorporated into egg or fish dishes.

**CAUTION: Avoid eating plants growing in soils that may be contaminated: research has indicated that perennial sow-thistle accumulates lead from contaminated soils.**[20]

# Spring beauty
## (*Claytonia perfoliata*)

The generic name *Claytonia* honours John Clayton (1694-1773), who was born in England but moved to Virginia, where he became one of North America's first botanists. Spring beauty, also known as winter purslane, is an interesting annual plant that is native to the Pacific coast of North America. It was used by miners as a fresh salad vegetable during the 1849 Gold Rush in California, earning it the alternative common name of miners' lettuce.

The plant was first introduced to Kew Gardens in Britain in 1794 by the botanist Archibald Menzies of Scotland, who also introduced the Douglas fir. It is a useful source of omega-3 fatty acids for those who do not eat oily fish.

## Appearance and habitat

Spring beauty was grown as a salad vegetable but has escaped cultivation and turns up as a weed plant, often in plant pots and particularly on damp, sandy soils. It grows best in cool, shady positions and is surprisingly frost hardy. The first leaves are usually heart-shaped, but then it forms a rosette of stalked, oval-shaped leaves. Later, usually between April and June in Britain (although earlier in its native California), it produces clusters of tiny, five-petalled, white flowers held on a succulent green, platter-like bract.

## Uses

The crisp, succulent leaves can be harvested as required throughout the winter and early spring. Treat them gently as, like those of spinach, they can bruise easily. They do not have a particularly strong flavour but are appreciated for their crisp texture. Unlike many other weeds the plant is still good to eat when in flower, and the flowers held in the decorative bracts make a really unusual addition to the salad bowl. It can also be boiled like spinach.

If it is sowing itself around rather too freely you can dig it into the ground before it flowers as a green manure.

## Related plants

*Claytonia sibirica*, the pink purslane, also originates from the North American west coast but, as the specific name suggests, it is also found in Siberia. It has naturalised in damp woodland and shady streams in Europe. It is virtually evergreen. The leaves are edible but have a somewhat acrid taste best disguised with a robust salad dressing.

*Claytonia caroliniana* is a dainty forest species of eastern North America. It produces small root tubers which are used by the Chilcotin people of British Columbia as potato substitutes. The delightfully named blinks, *Montia fontana*, is a widespread annual plant found in damp places from the tropics to the arctic. The tiny flowers remain tightly shut in dull weather. It has mild-tasting, succulent leaves that are pleasant in salads.

CAUTION: As with brooklime (see box, page 67), be careful with plants gathered from areas where liver fluke may be a problem.

# Stinging nettle
## (*Urtica dioica*)

A nettle pudding, made by mixing nettles and other wild leaves with barley flour, salt and water, is thought to have been one of the first dishes eaten in Britain. Nettles were widely used as both a vegetable, with the young spring greens made into soups and potages, and for their supposed medicinal properties. Gerard's *Herbal* of 1597 observed that nettles were used for conditions such as kidney diseases and lung ailments, and noted that the seeds "provoke lust". In his diary, Samuel Pepys reported on 25th February 1661 that he ate nettle porridge and considered it "very good".

A popular nettle-eating contest in Dorset evolved into the World Nettle Eating Championships. Competitors were given 60cm (2') lengths of nettles from which they plucked and ate the leaves. After an hour the bare stalks were measured; in 2010 the winner was found to have eaten more than 22.5m (74') of nettles. The event takes place in summer, when the nettles are really past their best for eating and can be quite bitter. The high iron content of the nettles tends to turn the mouth black and some competitors suffer facial paralysis.

The Nettle Warrior event in Staffordshire, in comparison, may be more energetic but less distasteful. It sees runners compete over a 13-km (8-mile) course through a number of obstacles, including cargo nets, muddy bogs and 2.1m (7')-high stinging nettles.

Nettles are a surprisingly good source of protein compared with other vegetables, and have been found to contain 16 different amino acids. They have been used to produce a form of vegetable protein similar to tofu, which is made from soy. They cannot, however, be considered complete proteins. Perhaps unsurprisingly, experiments in which rats were fed exclusively on nettle protein found that they failed to achieve normal growth.[21] It is, of course, unlikely that anyone would advocate a diet solely of nettles; however, the eccentric Cornish vicar Rev. F. W. Densham, who died in 1953, was said to have subsisted for many years on nettles and porridge. Nettles contain high levels of many vitamins and minerals such as zinc, iron and magnesium. The dietary fibre content varies from 9 to 21 per cent. The seeds contain the essential fatty acids linoleic acid and α-linolenic acid.[22]

## Appearance and habitat

Widely found in habitats associated with humans, such as farmyards and gardens, the stinging nettle grows most profusely on fertile, phosphate-rich soils. It is common throughout northern Europe and much of Asia, and in Canada and the USA. It is one of the most easily recognisable of plants, by touch even if not by sight. The plants are herbaceous perennials and usually grow to around 1m (3') tall but can be as much as twice that on moist, rich soils. The deep-green leaves are roughly heart-shaped with toothed margins. The green, catkin-like flowers, which open from June to August, are pollinated by the wind. Plants have tough, yellow, rhizomatous roots that can spread widely to form dense colonies.

The leaves and stem surfaces have stinging hairs known as trichomes, which if touched will break and release chemicals into the skin. The active substances are histamine, acetylcholine and 5-hydroxytrytamine. They cause pain, reddening of the skin and the formation of whitish weals. The effect is usually short-lived but can persist for 24 hours or more, and individual reactions vary greatly in their severity. The sap of dock leaves is considered to be a natural remedy for nettle stings, although the scientific evidence for this is limited. Fortunately, cooking or freezing nettles neutralises the sting so that they can then be eaten safely.

## Uses

The seeds are edible for humans and have an interesting, almost nutty flavour. They can be scattered over pizzas or used in risottos and soups. By the time nettles are seeding they have usually lost most of their sting so you may find that you are able to harvest them without gloves.

Gloves are essential when harvesting young nettles. They are best picked as young as possible, and before the end of June when they start to come into flower. By flowering time cystoliths (gritty particles made of calcium carbonate) are starting to form in the leaves, making them unpleasant to eat. As soon as they start to flower cut the nettles down to ground level. The tops can be stuffed into large buckets or barrels of water to rot down as is done with comfrey. Left for 2-3 weeks this will result in a high-quality plant fertiliser to use with crops such as tomatoes. Leaving the roots will ensure that the nettles spring up again, so long as the soil is still reasonably moist, so you can have a second crop of young leaves.

Both leaves and young shoots can be gathered. By earthing up the nettles in springtime they can be blanched like seakale. The most common use is for soups but nettle purée is still eaten in springtime in Italy, as it is supposed to be excellent for cleansing the blood.

Nettles have a fresh but not particularly strong taste and so can be steamed as a simple green vegetable, or are easy to use in omelettes and risottos. Irish nettle haggis is made from a purée of nettles, leeks, cabbage, bacon and oatmeal formed into a mound, wrapped in muslin, and boiled.

Nettle cordials are easily made and can be used in the cocktail known as a nettle gimlet, created by Tony Conigliaro for the Zetter Townhouse in London. It is made with one part of the cordial to two parts gin and garnished with a twist of lime zest. Nettles are used in some cheeses including Cornish Yarg, a modern British cheese matured in a wrapping of nettles.

Some reports suggest that in Roman times whipping yourself with nettles was used as a way to keep warm or to treat aching joints. For those not partial to self-flagellation, simply rubbing affected joints with nettle leaves could be tried. People in many parts of the world still use nettles as a remedy for arthritis, and experiments at the University of Plymouth lend some support to this use.[23] However, another study looking at people with osteoarthritis of the knee showed no significant reduction in pain for participants using stinging nettle leaves compared to those using dead-nettle leaves.[24]

The nettle is used as a natural dye-plant for wool and other natural fibres. The roots give a yellow dye, while shoots and leaves are used for a yellowish-green colour. Nettle string is tough and resistant, and ideal for horticultural use. It was formerly used by archers for bowstrings. To obtain the fibres from nettles you ideally need something like an old bathtub in which to soak the stems for 12 hours. The water is then changed and soaking continues until the soft green parts have rotted away.

You can, if you want, make some twine for the garden on a small scale. Cut several mature stems, and strip all the leaves from the stalks. Press and roll the nettle stalk between your fingers until it breaks. On the stalk is a coating of long, deep-green fibres. Strip these fibres carefully from the stalk so as not to break them. Look for long fibres and try to discard any that are too short or too fine. To form into string take two strands, one in the left and one in the right hand. Roll the right-hand strand clockwise between thumb and forefinger. The fibres should be pressed together in a clockwise corkscrew pattern. Lace the right strand counter-clockwise over the left strand, until the two strands fuse into one string. The fibres, trying to unwind, hit the other strand and stay together, forming a single string. Add extra fibres as needed as you go along.

## Related species

The Roman nettle, *Urtica pilulifera*, is a shorter-growing, annual species. The female flowers occur in interesting globular clusters. Another annual species is the small nettle, *U. urens*, which flowers from June to September. These species can be used as the common stinging nettle; however, some others are best avoided. *U. chamaedryoides* is an American species. It is fairly nondescript in appearance, with small leaves, but has been called 'fireweed' because of the intense burning sensation the plants elicit.

**CAUTION: The stings of the New Zealand endemic tree nettle (*U. ferox*) are particularly vicious and have been known to kill dogs, horses and at least one man.**

## Nettle and blackcurrant leaf cordial

Approximate preparation time: 1 hour plus infusing overnight

100g (3½oz) young nettle tops
100g (3½oz) blackcurrant leaves
570ml (20fl oz / 1 pint) water
1kg (2lb 3oz) sugar
40g (1½oz) citric acid

1  Rinse the nettles and blackcurrant leaves and put in a saucepan with the water. Bring to the boil, then turn off the heat and leave to infuse overnight.

2  Strain the liquid through muslin and return to a cleaned pan.

3  Add the sugar and citric acid and heat gently until the sugar is dissolved, then boil rapidly for a few minutes. Pour into sterile glass bottles and seal.

# Nettle risotto

2 tbsp olive oil

1 onion, chopped

400g (14oz) young nettles

300g (10½oz) Arborio rice

1.5 litres (55fl oz / 2¾ pints) chicken or vegetable stock

100g (3½oz) Parmesan cheese, grated

1  Heat the olive oil in a large saucepan. Add the onion and allow to soften for a few minutes.

2  Rinse the nettles, add to the pan and fry gently for 5 minutes.

3  Add the rice and stir well then just cover with a few ladlefuls of stock. As the rice absorbs the stock, add more liquid a ladleful at a time. Keep stirring to free any sticky grains from the bottom of the saucepan.

4  Once the rice is cooked remove the pan from the heat and stir in the cheese. Serve straight away.

# Nettle rissoles

Serves 4
Approximate preparation time: 30 minutes

200g (7oz) nettle leaves

1 onion, chopped

Knob of butter, plus butter or bacon fat to fry rissoles

100g (3½oz) oatmeal

2 eggs

2 tbsp Parmesan cheese, grated

1  Wash the nettles thoroughly, put in a pan and cook gently without added water for 4-5 minutes. Drain well.

2  Fry the onion in butter, add the nettles and cook for 5 minutes.

3  Allow to cool a little, then stir in the oatmeal, eggs and cheese and shape into rissoles. Fry in bacon fat or butter until golden.

# Nettle soup

Serves 4-6
Approximate preparation time: 30 minutes

1 large onion, chopped

50g (1¾oz) butter or olive oil

400g (14oz) potatoes, chopped into small chunks

400g (14oz) young nettles

1 litre (35fl oz / 1¾ pints) chicken or vegetable stock

Ground black pepper

1  Soften the onion in the fat in a large saucepan for 5 minutes.

2  Add the potatoes to the onion.

3  Rinse the nettles and add to the pan.

4  Pour in the stock and a sprinkle of pepper. Simmer for around 15 minutes until the potatoes are soft. Liquidise and serve with crusty bread.

# Nettle tart

Serves 6
Approximate preparation time: 1 hour

200g (7oz) shortcut pastry (if making this yourself, try mixing the dough with beer instead of water)

2 large handfuls of nettle tops

1 onion, chopped

1 tsp olive oil or knob butter

2 eggs

1 tsp Tewkesbury mustard

250ml/ (9fl oz) milk and cream combined

50g (1¾oz) cheese, grated

1  Roll out the pastry and use to line a 20cm (8") flan ring. Put into the fridge to rest for half an hour, then bake blind in a medium oven (180°C / 350°F / Gas Mark 4) for 10-15 minutes.

2  Blanch the nettle tops in boiling salted water for a couple of minutes. Drain.

3  Gently fry the onion in oil or butter until soft.

4  Beat the eggs with mustard and the milk-and-cream mixture.

5  Put the nettles and onion in the bottom of the pastry case, top with the cheese and pour over the egg and cream mixture. Return to the oven and cook for around 30 minutes until golden.

# Sweet violet
## (*Viola odorata*)

Violets have been grown since classical times for their flowers and for the oil that can be extracted from their petals for use in perfumes. The Romans were fond of violet-flavoured wine, and the lyric poet Horace criticised his countrymen for spending more time growing violets than tending to their olives.

In medieval times violets were made into a creamy pudding with almond milk thickened with rice flour. In the Tudor era both flowers and leaves were included in 'grand salletts' or 'salmagundis', which were large mixed salad dishes made up of assorted vegetables, fruit and sliced roast meats served on a bed of lettuce. Violets may not be as nutritious as olives but they can provide a useful winter source of vitamin C.

## Appearance and habitat

The sweet violet is a much-prized woodland plant whose early, fragrant flowers make springtime woodland walks such a pleasure. The flowers are most often violet-purple but a number of different colour forms have been selected for cultivation in gardens, including white and rose-red.

In the garden, violets are not always such an unreserved pleasure as they are in woodlands, as the long creeping stolons and dense leafy growth means that they can swamp more delicate spring bulbs and plants. They set seed generously and can quickly colonise a flower border as well as hedgerows, churchyards and scrubland.

Sugar-frosting sweet violet flowers.

The common dog violet.

## Uses

The heart-shaped leaves do not have a particularly strong taste but are useful in winter salads, or can be cooked and eaten as a green vegetable. They can be dipped in batter and fried then served with sugar and lemon juice.

Fresh violet flowers look attractive scattered over chocolate cakes or can be used to make a beautiful syrup for pouring over ice cream. They can be crystallised by dipping the flowers first into beaten egg white and then into a bowl of fine sugar. Use a small paintbrush to ensure that all parts of the flower are covered. Allow them to dry thoroughly then store in an air-tight box, where they can be kept for several days. Nibble as a sweet treat, or use to decorate cakes and desserts as well as chocolates such as violet creams.

## Related species

There are many different violets and the species tend to be quite promiscuous so that various hybrids can arise which can make positive identification challenging. None, however, are poisonous. Common dog violet (*Viola riviniana*), an unscented species, is the most widespread. Wild pansies (*V. tricolor*) are also edible and the flowers make a really attractive, albeit unexpected, addition to salads.

CAUTION: Eating large quantities of violets is not recommended as they have a high saponin content.

## Medieval violet pudding

Serves about 4
Approximate preparation time: 30 minutes plus time to set

2 cups violet petals, finely chopped

285ml (10fl oz / ½ pint) water

4 tbsp rice flour

570ml (20fl oz / 1 pint) milk

100g (3½oz) ground almonds

150ml (5½fl oz) double cream

100g (3½oz) sugar

**1**  Add the violets to the water in a saucepan. Bring to the boil and cook for minute or so, then drain. (Reserve the water if you want to make a violet syrup.)

**2**  Mix the rice flour to a paste with a little of the milk. Bring the rest of the milk to the boil, mix with the rice paste and cook gently over a low heat, stirring until it begins to thicken.

**3**  Add the ground almonds and cook over a very low heat until thick.

**4**  Add the violets, cream and sugar and heat until the sugar has dissolved. Pour into glass bowls or ramekins and allow to cool.

## Sweet violet syrup

Approximate preparation time: 1 hour, plus infusing overnight

2 cups violet petals

285ml (10fl oz / ½ pint) boiling water

680g (1lb 8oz) sugar

**1**  Put the petals in a glass or china bowl. Pour the boiling water over the flowers and leave to infuse overnight.

**2**  The next day strain the water into a saucepan and stir in the sugar. Bring the liquid to a gentle rolling boil until thick and syrupy. Bottle in sterile glass jars, and seal.

# White dead-nettle
## (*Lamium album*)

Also known as bee nettle, as the nectar-rich flowers are regularly visited by bees, white dead-nettle is a common and easily recognisable plant. It has a long history of use as a pot-herb in France and Sweden. Herbal teas made from the flowers show active antioxidant properties.

## Appearance and habitat

A familiar plant in hedgerows, gardens and on waste ground, white dead-nettle has stinging-nettle-shaped leaves that have no sting. Native to Europe and western Asia, it is a perennial plant that grows to around 50cm (1'8") tall. From April, often right through till midwinter, it carries quantities of white-hooded flowers.

## Uses

Young leaves can be eaten raw in mixed salads, but once the plants start to come into flower they can become rather chewy. To serve dead-nettles as spring greens, gather the young shoots and leaves, thoroughly wash them and put them in a pan with a knob of butter, a splash of lemon juice and some black pepper. Cook over a medium heat for about 10 minutes.

To prepare the flowers for dead-nettle tea, pick them when freshly opened and lay them on a tray lined with kitchen paper. Dry in an airing cupboard for 2-3 days, turning them occasionally until brittle. Store in an airtight container in a cool, dark place. To make the tea, put 1 tsp dried flowers in a teapot. Pour over 285ml (10fl oz / ½ pint) boiling water. Cover and infuse for 5 minutes. Strain and flavour with lemon or honey if liked.

## Related species

Red dead-nettle (*Lamium purpureum*), henbit dead-nettle (*L. amplexicaule*) and yellow archangel (*L. galeobdolon*) can all be treated in the same way.

# Wild carrot
## (*Daucus carota*)

The domesticated carrot has been a familiar vegetable since at least classical times. It is thought to have been introduced to Europe by the tenth century. The wild form, which may occur as a weed in gardens, rarely produces a substantial root but the young leaves can be used as nutritious spring greens.

## Appearance and habitat

Wild carrot is a very variable plant that can grow as an annual or biennial. The most commonly encountered as a wild plant or weed is subspecies *carota*, which has thin, lightly hairy leaves and flower umbels that contract and become concave in fruit. The alternative common name of bird's-nest is derived from the shape of the seedheads. The taproot is usually thin and white. The cultivated carrot, with thick fleshy taproot, is subspecies *sativus*.

## Uses

Wild carrot is a good choice of plant for a meadow garden as the white, lacy flowers are very attractive in late summer and are much loved by bees, butterflies and hoverflies. They are also edible and can be used to add interest to mixed salads, having a mild, but distinctly carroty flavour. Young carrot leaves can also be used but they become bitter as they mature. If you grow carrots it is worth saving the seedling leaves obtained when thinning out, and adding them to a salad.

You can, of course, also eat the roots of wild carrot, but they are rarely fleshy enough to make a worthwhile meal.

**CAUTION: Make absolutely certain that you have identified this plant correctly, as it is similar in leaf and flower to related plants, such as cowbane (*Cicuta virosa*) and fool's parsley (*Aethusa cynapium*), which are extremely poisonous.**

# Wild garlic
## (*Allium ursinum*)

Wild garlic is also known as ramsons, wood garlic or bear's garlic; the last name and the specific name *ursinum* referring to the fact that the European brown bear has a taste for the bulbs and will dig them up to eat. An ancient English rhyme exhorted people to 'Eat leeks in Lide and ramsoms in May, and all the year after physicians may play.' Lide is an old word for March, suggesting that if you started your year off by consuming plenty of alliums you would not need to trouble your doctor later.

Wild garlic has been eaten for thousands of years and has long been considered to have medicinal properties. Like cultivated garlic (*Allium sativum*) it is often said to be effective at lowering cholesterol levels, and so useful in treating heart disease, but such claims do not have strong scientific backing.[25] The leaves of wild garlic are higher in antioxidants than the bulbs or flowers.

## Appearance and habitat

A common bulbous plant usually found in woodland on damp, rich soils, wild garlic is widely distributed throughout most of Europe. The rounded heads of starry white flowers light up the woodland floor from April to June.

It often grows in large colonies which, when in leaf, can be smelt for quite a distance. If you deliberately plant the bulbs in the garden they may well disappear without a trace, but if the conditions suit them you could soon decide that you have too much of a good thing.

## Uses

Wild garlic can be substituted for garlic cloves in many dishes. The taste is not as strong as the scent would lead you to expect. The rich green colour is attractive in omelettes, and it can be used instead of cabbage in bubble and squeak. It has a great affinity with fish and is excellent in tomato-based dishes.

The flowers look appealing scattered over salads, giving a sweeter garlicky flavour. Young green seedpods can be cut while they are still developing and used in pestos.

A wild garlic butter can be made by beating a generous handful of finely chopped wild garlic leaves into 100g (3½oz) butter with a squeeze of lemon juice. This can be used to make garlic bread, added to mashed or cooked new potatoes or melted on to grilled fish or steaks.

Mix chopped wild garlic with cream cheese to make a tasty dip, or use in place of basil when making pesto.

## Related species

Field garlic, *Allium oleraceum*, is found on drier ground, growing in the open and usually on limestone. It has narrow leaves, more like the culinary onion, and is taller, growing to around 60-70cm (2'-2'4"). Three-cornered leek, *A. triquetrum*, is a native of the western

CAUTION: The broad, dark green leaves look similar to those of lily-of-the-valley (*Convallaria majalis*), all parts of which are poisonous, so be sure that you can distinguish between the two plants. Use your hands and nose to guide you: lily-of-the-valley leaves have a firm, plastic texture and a fresh, grassy smell, whereas wild garlic leaves are much more pliable and have that unmistakable garlic scent.

As with cultivated onions and other members of the *Allium* genus, wild garlic contains n-propyl disulphide, which in large quantities can cause the breakdown of red blood cells leading to anaemia. There are no reports of human poisoning but dogs and cats seem to be more sensitive and should not be given onions or wild garlic.

Mediterranean region but was introduced to Britain in 1752 and is now widely naturalised there and elsewhere. It can be invasive in gardens, although it grows prolifically only in areas with reasonably mild winters. As the name suggests, it has a triangular stem. The white flowers have a green stripe down the centre of each petal. Both leaves and flowers can be added to salads.

Crow garlic, *A. vineale*, is an invasive species on sandy soils and dry grassland. The chive-like leaves die back before the flowers emerge. Flower heads are composed of greenish-pink flowers interspersed with small green or purple bulbils which drop off and grow into new plants. The leaves can be gathered in spring and used as chives. The bulbils make an interesting addition to salads, or scattered over soups instead of croutons.

## Wild garlic pesto

Serve as a dressing or with bread
Approximate preparation time: 15 minutes

200g (7oz) wild garlic leaves
100g (3½oz) pine nuts
200g (7oz) Parmesan cheese, grated
Olive oil

Pesto is traditionally prepared by pounding the ingredients in a marble mortar with a wooden pestle. Wooden pestles are better than stone ones as they are less likely to smear the leaves into a green slime, but you can, of course, grind the ingredients together in any way you prefer.

1  Pound the wild garlic leaves and pine nuts together to form a paste and then work in the cheese and a little olive oil to form a thick sauce.

Serve with pasta or new boiled potatoes or as a spread on fresh crusty bread.

## Wild garlic soup

Serves 4
Approximate preparation time: 20 minutes

1 large potato, diced (about 200g (7oz))
1 litre (35fl oz / 1¾ pints) chicken or vegetable stock
400g (14oz) wild garlic
2 tbsp sour cream

1  Boil the potato in the stock until soft.

2  Add the wild garlic and cook for a further minute or two.

3  Blend until smooth and serve with a swirl of sour cream if liked.

# Wild lettuce
## (*Lactuca* spp.)

All species of wild lettuce ooze a milky sap if the leaves or stems are broken. This reminded the ancient Egyptians of semen and they considered lettuce to be an aphrodisiac. It was closely associated with the fertility god Min. In fact, lettuce is more likely to have the opposite effect as it contains the drug lactucarium, which at one time was used as a sedative. The Roman author Pliny wrote about a type of lettuce known as 'the eunuch's lettuce', which was supposed to cause impotence, and in the seventeenth century lettuce was recommended as suitable for monks and nuns to eat. Most lettuces provide useful quantities of vitamins A and K.

## Appearance and habitat

There are around 100 species of wild lettuces. They are mostly tall, weedy-looking annuals, somewhat similar in appearance to sow-thistles. The leaves usually have jagged edges and a bluish-green bloom to them, and are often spiny underneath. They usually have tiny yellow daisy-like flowers arranged in open branching clusters from July to September. *Lactuca alpina* is an exception, having blue flowers. The great lettuce, *L. virosa*, is the most widely distributed, often occurring on disturbed ground.

## Uses

The very first leaves to emerge in the spring can be used in salads, but leaves quickly become unpleasantly bitter and are only acceptable eating if boiled, with a couple of changes of water during cooking. However, most people prefer the taste of modern cultivated lettuces, which were developed from the species *L. sativa*.

# Wintercress
## (*Barbarea vulgaris*)

Wintercress, as the common name implies, is a useful source of greens over the winter period. In fact, the genus name *Barbarea* also alludes to this, as it is derived from the traditional feast day of St Barbara, which is on 4th December. The leaves are a valuable source of vitamin C with a content of 130mg per 100g.

## Appearance and habitat

A member of the cabbage family (Brassicaceae), wintercress is a biennial or perennial plant with rosettes of distinctive dark green, glossy leaves. It flowers from May to September with tall stems of small yellow flowers. If you remove the flowering stems when they start to shoot, adding water if the soil is dry, the plant will respond by producing a fresh crop of large basal leaves.

## Uses

The leaves can be cut at any time and used in salads or as a green vegetable. They have a strong peppery taste, like an intense form of watercress, and will definitely warm up the tastebuds in a winter salad. In parts of Italy the leaves are used to make a broth that is considered to be a remedy for respiratory diseases. The unopened flower buds can be used like those of broccoli.

## Related species

Early wintercress (*Barbarea intermedia*), a native of south and central Europe, usually flowers before *B. vulgaris*. The American land cress (*B. verna*) in fact originates in south-west Europe but is often used as a vegetable in the USA, where it may be known as creasy greens. It is a useful, hardy crop, forming neat rosettes of leaves. It generally flowers from May to July.

# Yarrow
## (*Achillea millefolium*)

The botanical name *Achillea* commemorates the classical hero Achilles, who was said to have used yarrow to staunch bleeding on the battlefields of Troy. The plant is still used today in Romania as a herbal remedy for circulatory disorders. Yarrow is a good source of many minerals, including calcium, potassium and phosphorus, particularly when growing on heavy soils.

## Appearance and habitat

Yarrow is a perennial plant that grows to around 40cm (1'4") tall, spreading by seed but also by creeping underground rhizomes. It is common in rough grassland, lawns and verges with a preference for drier conditions. It is very tolerant of mowing. The alternative common name of milfoil is, like the specific name *millefolium* (thousand leaves), a reference to the much-divided, lacy leaves. When crushed, yarrow leaves have a bitter, chrysanthemum-like smell.

Yarrow flowers throughout the summer and sometimes well into winter, with flat heads of many white or pink flowers that attract a variety of insects. There are a number of different-coloured ornamental selections available in the nursery trade. The dead flowerheads are persistent in winter and bring an interesting sculptural quality to the garden when dusted with frost or snow.

## Uses

Yarrow can be eaten raw in salads but it is rather chewy and bitter so is something of an acquired taste. To use as a cooked green vegetable, strip the leaves from the stems and boil for around 10 minutes. Drain off the water, add a knob of butter and fry for a further couple of minutes.

Yarrow makes a soothing tea.

CAUTION: Before eating yarrow, be sure that you can identify it correctly. It should not be confused with poisonous plants with white umbels of flowers, such as hemlock and cowbane.

Handling yarrow can cause skin irritation in susceptible people.

Yarrow tea is a traditional remedy for the common cold. It may not be scientifically proven as a cure, but the tea is easily made by infusing a couple of fresh or dried yarrow leaves in boiling water for a few minutes. Remove the leaves then serve with a slice of lemon or lime. It makes a soothing bedtime drink.

Experiments have shown that the presence of yarrow can inhibit the build-up of parasites in bird's nests.[26] If you keep poultry it may be worth borrowing this idea and using a few handfuls of yarrow in the nest boxes.

## Achilles' heels

Serves about 4
Approximate preparation time: 30 minutes

Large handful of yarrow leaves

6 spring onions, chopped

30g (1oz) butter

200g (7oz) potato, boiled and mashed with a splash of milk

Oil to fry patties

1 Boil the leaves in salted water for 10 minutes then drain.

2 Fry the spring onions and drained leaves in the butter for a few minutes, then add to the mashed potato and mix thoroughly.

3 Form into small patties and fry until golden. Serve with thick rashers of grilled back bacon.

# Yellow sorrel
## (*Oxalis corniculata*)

Yellow sorrel has been known in Britain since the Middle Ages. It is a prolific garden weed which seems to have been widely spread in the nursery trade. In central India it has long been used as a famine food by communities such as the Sahariya tribe. The protein and lipid contents of the leaves are higher than those of many other green vegetables, and the level of iron in the leaves is three times the level found in cultivated spinach leaves.

## Appearance and habitat

Seemingly innocuous seedlings with green or bronze trefoil leaves like miniature clovers may be introduced to the garden with plants purchased from a garden centre. The small, pale yellow flowers rapidly set seed, forming chubby seedpods from which the seeds are flung to all parts of the garden. In good soil the plants send down a deep taproot and spread by creeping stems which root at the nodes, as well as by seed.

## Control

Plants will grow in the tiny cracks of paving and in the mortar of brick walls. They are quite difficult to hand-weed as they tend to snap off at ground level, leaving the taproot to regenerate. It is best to ensure the soil is moist first and then to prise the root out with a hand fork or daisy grubber.

## Uses

The leaves have an excellent sharp lemon tang and are useful for scattering over salads to enliven more bland-tasting leaves. Try a few in egg sandwiches as an alternative to cress. The flowers and seedpods can also be used in salads.

## Related species

The Bermuda buttercup (*Oxalis pes-caprae*) comes not from Bermuda but from South Africa. It is a widespread weed of cultivated and wasteland. In California and parts of Australia it is considered a noxious weed. It is the largest of the yellow-flowered sorrels and is particularly resistant to herbicides but is not frost-hardy. It has a fairly chubby, edible underground bulb. Double-flowered forms are commonly found.

A native of South America, pink oxalis (*O. articulata*) has hairy leaflets covered in orange or brown dots. It is often planted as an ornamental but spreads rapidly and with great determination. A demure-looking relative, the wood sorrel (*O. acetosella*) grows in shady places. It has white, or occasionally pink, nodding flowers. As with other *Oxalis* species the leaves are sometimes used as a salad vegetable and in green sauces. Crushed with sugar and water they can make an interesting country lemonade. However, caution must be exercised owing to the high oxalic acid content.

CAUTION: Do remember that all *Oxalis* species are high in oxalic acid. Oxalic acid is found in many commonly eaten fruit and vegetables, including grapefruit and spinach, but if eaten in large quantities can cause kidney stones. It is sensible therefore to eat all *Oxalis* species sparingly.

# Glossary

**Annual** A plant that completes its lifecycle in one growing season.

**Antioxidant** A molecule capable of inhibiting the oxidation of other molecules.

**Biennial** A plant that flowers and seeds in the second season after germination.

**Biological control** The control of pests and weeds by the use of other living organisms.

**Blanch** To deprive of light so that leaves become pale and less bitter. Also in culinary use: to boil for just a few seconds.

**Brassica** A member of the cabbage family.

**Cultivar** Any cultivated variety of a plant. The term is often used interchangeably with 'variety'.

**Deciduous** A plant that sheds its leaves annually.

**Fodder crop** Crop used as food for cattle and other livestock.

**Forage** (n.) Food for horses and cattle; also (vb.) to search for food.

**Genus** A category in plant classification between family and species.

**Legume** Any plant of the pea family, Fabaceae (Leguminosae), especially peas and beans.

**Loam** A term usually used imprecisely to denote a rich soil with a balanced mix of clay, sand and humus.

**Mucilaginous** Thick or sticky.

**Mulch** A material applied in a layer to the soil surface.

**Node** The point on a stem where one or more leaves, shoots or flowers are attached.

**Perennial** Any plant living for at least three growing seasons.

**Phototoxic** Having a toxic effect that is triggered by exposure to sunlight.

**Phytotoxic** Poisonous to plants.

**Pollen** The male sex cells produced by the stamens.

**Pollination** The transfer of pollen from anthers to stigmas.

**Receptacle** The enlarged end of the stem from which the floral parts derive.

**Rhizomatous** Having a specialised stem under or close to the soil surface, from which new roots and stems may develop.

**Species** A category in plant classification containing very similar individuals.

**Stolon** An above-ground stem that gives rise to new plants at its tip or at intermediate nodes.

**Strewing herb** A plant that was scattered over the floor to fragrance the room and repel fleas.

**Symbiotic** A close, mutually beneficial, relationship between different biological species.

**Temperate** A region or climate without extremes of temperature.

**Umbel** A flat-topped inflorescence with all of the flower stalks arising from the same point of the stem.

**Variety** A grouping of plants having distinctive features that persist through successive generations.

# Notes*

## Part 1

CHAPTER 1
1. Dittmer, H. J. (1937). 'A quantitative study of the roots and root hairs of a winter rye plant (*Secale cereale*)'. *American Journal of Botany* 24(7): 417-20
2. Schweizer, E. E. (1983). 'Common lambsquarters (*Chenopodium album*) interference in sugar beets (*Beta vulgaris*)'. *Weed Science (USA)* 31: 5-8.
3. Weston, L. A. (2005). 'History and current trends in the use of allelopathy for weed management'. *HortTechnology* 13: 529-34.
4. Cooper, M. R. and Johnson, A. W. (1984). *Poisonous Plants in Britain and their Effects on Animals and Man*. The Stationery Office, London.
5. Smith, J. G. (1976). 'Influence of crop background on aphids and other phytophagous insects on Brussels sprouts'. *Annals of Applied Biology* 83(1): 1-13.
6. Finch, S. and Collier, R. (2003). 'Insects can see clearly now the weeds have gone'. *Biologist* 50(3): 132-5.

CHAPTER 2
1. Dunnett, N. and Hitchmough, J. (2001). 'First in, last out'. *The Garden* 126(3): 182-3.

CHAPTER 3
1. Rugman, F. and Meecham, J. (1983). '*Mercurialis perennis* (dog's mercury) poisoning: a case of mistaken identity'. *British Medical Journal* 287: 1924.
2. Owen, J. (2009). 'Ancient death-smile potion decoded?' *National Geographic News*. http://news.nationalgeographic.com/news/2009/06/090602-smiling-death-potion.html.
3. Curhan, G. C., Willett, W. C., Rimm, E. B. et al. (1993). 'A prospective study of dietary calcium and other nutrients and the risk of symptomatic kidney stones'. *New England Journal of Medicine* 328: 833-8.
4. Holmes, R. P. and Kennedy, M. (2000). 'Estimation of the oxalate content of foods and daily oxalate intake'. *Kidney International* 57: 1662-7.
5. Akbar, K. F., Hale, W. H. G., Headley, A. D. et al. (2006). 'Heavy metals contamination of roadside soils of northern England'. *Soil & Water Research* 1(4): 158-63.

## Part 2

1. Halvorsen, B. L., Holte, K., Myhrstad, M. C. W. et al. (2002). 'A systematic screening of total antioxidants in dietary plants'. *The Journal of Nutrition* 132(3): 461-71.
2. Evans, I. A., Widdop, B., Jones, R. S. et al. (1971). 'The possible human hazard of the naturally occurring bracken carcinogen'. *Biochemical Journal* 124(2): 29-30.
3. Rasmussen, L. H. (2003). 'Ptaquiloside – an environmental hazard? Occurrence and fate of a bracken (*Pteridium* sp.) toxin in terrestrial environments'. www.staff.kvl.dk/~lhr/Documents/Rasmussen%20Ptaquiloside%20-%20an%20environmental%20hazard.pdf.
4. Elwyn Hughes, R. (1990). 'The rise and fall of the "antiscorbutics": some notes on the traditional cures for "land scurvy"'. *Medical History* 34: 52-64.
5. Mayhew, H. (1861). *London Labour and the London Poor*. Volume 1. http://dl.tufts.edu/view_text.jsp?pid=tufts:MS004.002.052.001.00001.
6. www.guinnessworldrecords.com/records-1/most-leaves-on-a-clover/.
7. Tice, J. A., Ettinger, B., Ensrud, K. et al. (2003). 'Phytoestrogen supplements for

the treatment of hot flashes: the isoflavone clover extract study'. *Journal of the American Medical Association* 290(2): 207-14.

8    Frohne, D. and Pfänder, H. J. (1983). *A Colour Atlas of Poisonous Plants*. Wolfe, London.

9    Yildirim, E., Dursun, A. and Turan, M. (2001). 'Determination of the nutrition contents of the wild plants used as vegetables in Upper Çoruh valley'. *Turkish Journal of Botany* 25: 367-71.

10   Carlsson, R. and Hallqvist, C.-W. (1981). '*Atriplex hortensis* L.– revival of a spinach plant'. *Acta Agriculturae Scandinavica* 31(3): 229-34.

11   Abrams, S. A., Griffin, I. J., Hawthorne, K. M. et al. (2005). 'A combination of prebiotic short- and long-chain inulin-type fructans enhances calcium absorption and bone mineralization in young adolescents'. *American Journal of Clinical Nutrition* 82(2): 471-6.

12   Klimko, M., Antkowiak, M. and Nowińska, R. (2009). 'The influence of habitat conditions on anatomical structure of *Impatiens parviflora* DC (Balsaminaceae)'. *Botanika-Steciana* 13: 191-202.

13   Frohne, D. and Pfänder, H. J. (1983). *A Colour Atlas of Poisonous Plants*. Wolfe, London.

14   Becker, P. G. (2007). Bionic knotweed control. www.newtritionink.de/shop/pdf/english.pdf.

15   Rodríguez-Morán, M., Guerrero-Romero, F. and Lazcano-Burciaga, G. (1998). 'Lipid- and glucose-lowering efficacy of *Plantago psyllium* in type II diabetes'. *Journal of Diabetes and its Complications* 12(5): 273-8.

16   Simopoulos, A. P., Norman, H. A., Gillaspy, J. E. et al. (1992). 'Common purslane: a source of omega-3 fatty acids and antioxidants'. *Journal of the American College of Nutrition* 11(4): 374-82.

17   Haffner, K. and Remberg, S. F. (2006). 'Antioxidant-rich berries: plant food for better health'. *Chronica Horticulture* 46(2): 19-20.

18   Roman, I., Rusu, M. A., Puică, C. et al. (2010). 'Citotoxic effects of three species of *Epilobium* (Onagraceae) herbal extracts in rats'. *Studia Universitatis 'Vasile Goldiş'* 20(1): 19-23.

19   Xia, L. and You, J. (2011). 'The determination of amino acids composition of the traditional food Potentilla anserina L. root by high-performance liquid chromatography via fluorescent detection and mass spectrometry'. *International Journal of Food Science & Technology* 46(6): 1164-70.

20   Surat, W., Kruatrachue, M., Pokethitiyook, P. et al. (2008). 'Potential of *Sonchus arvensis* for the phytoremediation of lead-contaminated soil'. *International Journal of Phytoremediation* 10(4): 325-42.

21   Hughes, R. E., Ellery, P., Harry, T. et al. (1980). 'The dietary potential of the common nettle'. *Journal of the Science of Food and Agriculture* 31: 1279–86.

22   Guil-Guerrero, J. L., Rebolloso-Fuentes, M. M. and Torija Isasa, M. E. (2003). 'Fatty acids and carotenoids from stinging nettle (*Urtica dioica* L.)'. *Journal of Food Composition and Analysis* 16(2): 111-19.

23   Randall, C., Randall, H., Dobbs, F. et al. (2000). Randomized controlled trial of nettle sting for treatment of base-of-thumb pain. *Journal of Royal Society of Medicine* 93(6): 305-9.

24   De Silva, V. et al. (2010). 'Evidence for the efficacy of complementary and alternative medicines in the management of osteoarthritis: a systematic review'. *Rheumatology*, first published online 17.12.2010, doi:10.1093/rheumatology/keq379

25   Gardner, C. D., Lawson L. D., Block, E. et al. (2007). 'Effect of raw garlic vs commercial garlic supplements on plasma lipid concentrations in adults with moderate hypercholesterolemia; a randomized clinical trial'. *Archives of Internal Medicine* 167(4): 346-53.

26   Shutler, D. and Campbell, A. A. (2007). 'Experimental addition of greenery reduces flea loads in nests of a non-greenery using species, the tree swallow *Tachycineta bicolor*'. *Journal of Avian Biology* 38(1): 7-12.

# Bibliography

*A Colour Atlas of Poisonous Plants.* Dietrich Frohne and Hans Jürgen Pfänder (1983). Wolfe, London.

*Flora Britannica.* Richard Mabey (1997). Chatto & Windus, London.

*Food for Free.* Richard Mabey (2004). HarperCollins, Glasgow.

*The Forager Handbook.* Miles Irving (2009). Ebury Press, London.

*New Flora of the British Isles.* Clive Stace (2010). Cambridge University Press, Cambridge.

*The Organic Salad Garden.* Joy Larkcom (2001). Francis Lincoln, London.

*Poisonous Plants in Britain and their Effects on Animals and Man.* Marion Cooper and Anthony Johnson (1984). The Stationery Office, London.

*The Wild Flowers of the British Isles.* David Streeter (1998). Midsummer Books, London.

*Wild Food.* Roger Phillips (1983). Pan Macmillan, London.

# Index

Page numbers in **bold**
indicate where the main
information, uses and
recipes are to be found for
that plant. Page numbers in
*italic* refer to illustrations.